100

PROGR...

FOR T...

BBC MICROCOMPUTER

Other books published by Prentice-Hall International

BASIC PROGRAMMING ON THE BBC MICROCOMPUTER,
  Neil Cryer and Pat Cryer

BBC MICROCOMPUTER FOR BEGINNERS,
  Seamus Dunn and Valerie Morgan

GRAPHICS ON THE BBC MICROCOMPUTER,
  Neil Cryer, Pat Cryer and Andrew Cryer

100
PROGRAMS
FOR THE
BBC MICROCOMPUTER

John Gordon

MEDC, Paisley College, Scotland

Prentice/Hall PHI International

Englewood Cliffs, NJ London New Delhi Rio de Janeiro
Singapore Sydney Tokyo Toronto Wellington

Published in association with ACORNSOFT

Library of Congress Cataloging in Publication Data
Gordon, John, 1952—
  100 programs for the BBC microcomputer.

  1. Microcomputers—Programming. 2. Basic (Computer
program language) I. Title. II. Title: B.B.C.
microcomputer. III. Title: BBC microcomputer. IV. Title:
One hundred programs for the B.B.C. microcomputer.
QA76.6.G665 1983   001.64'2   83-6206

British Library Cataloguing in Publication Data

Gordon, John
  100 programs for the BBC microcomputer.
  1. Microcomputer—Programming   2. Basic:
  Computer program language
  I. Title
  001.64'2   QA76.6

  ISBN 0-13-634741-X

0-13-634741 X

0-13-634733 9 {CASSETTE}

Prentice-Hall International, Inc., *London*
Prentice-Hall of Australia Pty Ltd, *Sydney*
Prentice-Hall Canada, Inc., *Toronto*
Prentice-Hall of India Private Ltd, *New Delhi*
Prentice-Hall of Japan, Inc., *Tokyo*
Prentice-Hall of Southeast Asia Pte Ltd, *Singapore*
Prentice-Hall, Inc., *Englewood Cliffs, New Jersey*
Prentice-Hall do Brasil Ltda, *Rio de Janeiro*
Whitehall Books Ltd, *Wellington, New Zealand*

10 9 8 7 6 5 4 3

Printed in Great Britain by A. Wheaton & Co. Ltd., Exeter

To my Mother and Father

ADDENDA

The following changes should be made too
Program P18 - Monster Island:

Line 680, <u>insert</u> OR L=128 <u>after</u> IF L=224
Line 690, <u>insert</u> OR L=129 <u>after</u> IF L=225
Line 880, <u>insert</u> OR L=129 <u>after</u> IF L=225
Line 900, <u>insert</u> OR L=130 <u>after</u> IF L=226

CONTENTS

Preface   xi

SECTION 1   INTRODUCTION   2
    P1   Nitemare   8
    P2   Musak   10
    P3   Tunes   11
    P4   Pattern   14
    P5   Graph Plotting   16
    P6   Bouncing Ball 1   19
    P7   Bouncing Ball 2   20
    P8   Jimmy   21
    P9   Clock   23
    P10   Soft Keys— Program Development   26

SECTION 2   GAMES
    P11   Mastermind   27
    P12   Guess the Number   29
    P13   Reaction Test   31
    P14   Gobble   32
    P15   Tennis   35
    P16   Bombs   37
    P17   Bat'n'Moths   40
    P18   Monster Island   43
    P19   Battleships   46

SECTION 3   BUSINESS
    P20   Loan Repayment Period   50
    P21   Wordprocessor   52
    P22   Depreciation   56
    P23   Four-weekly Moving Average   58
    P24   Mailing List Creation   61
    P25   Mailing List Print   62
   P26, P27 and P28   Stock Control   63
          P26   Stock File Creation
          P27   Transaction File Creation
          P28   Stock File Update and Report
    P29   VAT Calculator   68
    P30   True Rate of Interest   69

SECTION 4   AT HOME

P31	Simple Tax Calculator	70
P32	Loan Repayments	73
P33	Monthly Accounts	75
P34	Conversion	78
P35	Birthday List	80
P36	Diary	82
P37, P38 and P39 Christmas Card List System		84

P37	Christmas Card List Creation	
P38	Christmas Card List Maintenance	
P39	Christmas Card List Print	

P40	Calendar	89
P41	Telephone List	91
P42	Investments	93

SECTION 5   PAINTING ON THE SCREEN

P43	Circles	94
P44	Interference	96
P45	Picture	97
P46	Pictures	98
P47	Zoom	102
P48	Worm	104
P49	Drawing	106
P50	MODE 7 Colours	107
P51	Writing Text At The Graphics Cursor	108
P52	Screen Dump	110

SECTION 6   DATA HANDLING PROGRAMS

P53	Pie Chart	112
P54	Bar Chart	114
P55	Mean and Standard Deviation	116
P56	Bubble Sort	119
P57	Shell Sort	121
P58	Merge	123
P59	Binary Search	125
P60	Permutations	127
P61	Combinations	128
P62	Least Squares	129

SECTION 7   RECREATION

P63	Number of Days	131
P64	Digital Clock	132
P65	Kitchen Timer	133
P66	Recipes	134
P67	Encoder	139
P68	Decoder	141

P69	The Game Of Life	143
P70	Biorhythms	146
P71	Anagrams	148
P72	Magic Matrix	149
P73	Dice	151
P74	Pools Program	152
P75	Shuffle	153

SECTION 8   THE SCIENCE LAB

P76	Number Base Conversion	155
P77	Colour Codes For Resistors	158
P78	Volumes of Solids	160
P79 and P80	Physics	163
	P79 Moment of Inertia	164
	P80 Focal Length	166
P81	Resistors	168
P82	Calculator	169
P83	Coordinate Converson	170

SECTION 9   MATHEMATICS

P84	Vectors	172
P85	Quadratic Equations	174
P86	Factorisation	176
P87	Factorial	178
P88	Polynomial Multiplication	180
P89	Jacobi Method for Solving Systems of Equations	182
P90	Greatest Common Divisor	186
P91	Matrix Multiplication	187
P92	Secant Method	189
P93	Method of Bisections	191
P94	Trapezoidal Rule	193
P95	Simpson's Rule	195

SECTION 10   PROGRAMS FOR THE SCHOOL

P96	Arithmetic Tutor	196
P97 and P98	French and German Tutorial	199
	P97 French Tutorial	
	P98 German Tutorial	
P99	Spelling	202
P100	Counting	205
* P101	School Report	207

*Bonus program.

```
10 REM PREFACE
20 REM This is where we say thanks to all
        those who helped in the
        production of  this volume.
30 MODE 7
40 PRINT "I  wish especially to mention
            the following individuals who
            have helped in various ways"
50 FOR I=1 TO 5
60 READ A$,B$
70 PRINT A$,B$
80 NEXT I
90 PRINT "I must also thank the reviewers
            of  this  book  for  their
            extremely helpful comments, and
            for the circle drawing routine
            which appears at various points
            in this volume"
100 PRINT "I  must  also  thank  Peter
            Williams, for starting me off
            on this project"
110 PRINT "Most of all, I can now get
            back to family life, now that
            this is the END"
120 NEW
130 DATA  Francis Campbell,for keying in
            some of the code
140 DATA  Hugh Pearson,for trying out the
            programs
150 DATA  The technical staff at MEDC,for
            many helpful words.
160 DATA  Teresa,for tea and sympathy
170 DATA  Jayne,for helping me with the
            games.
180 DATA  John Ferguson,for designing the
            PICONET network for the BBC
            micro
```

John Gordon
Paisley, 1983

100
PROGRAMS
FOR THE
BBC MICROCOMPUTER

INTRODUCTION

The BBC microcomputer has been with us now for a year or so,
and appears to have overcome its initial teething troubles.
It has now taken its place in the market as a rather
sophisticated low cost computer; in my opinion, it is the
best machine for its price.

This book represents about six month's work, although
perhaps it might be too strong to call it work. It can be
great fun to sit in front of a keyboard, getting a program
to work properly. It is also with a sense of achievement and
satisfaction that I present to you this selection of
computer programs.

I have, in my selection, attempted to answer the question
" What do you use a microcomputer for?" You will find
routines in this book which cover the use of micros at home,
in business, in school and for pleasure.

Before starting off on the programs themselves it is
worthwhile to consider the structure of the BBC micro and
the difference between different versions.

Model A or Model B

The BBC micro comes in two models, A and B. The majority
of tl programs in this book have been designed to run on
both models and thus only utilise model A features. It is
possible to upgrade many of these programs to take advan-
tage of the model B features, especially the graphics.

Operating Systems

As well as having two basic models, the BBC microcomputer
also comes with various versions of operating system (OS).
At the time of writing, there are OS 0.1, OS 1.0, OS 1.1 and
OS 1.2.

Each version of the operating system removed various bugs
and deficiencies in the older operating systems. I have
attempted to write the programs so they will work across the
various operating systems. But bear in mind they were
written on a machine under operating system 0.1. The main
problem is the switching off of the flashing cursor in the
various graphics programs.

Under OS 0.1 the correct line of code is
    VDU 23;8202;0;0;0;

In version 1.0 of the operating system
    VDU 23,1,0;0;0;0; will switch cursor off
    VDU 23,1,1;0;0;0; will switch cursor on.

Cassette Operating System (COS)

As well as having different OS's, the BBC micro also has different peripheral handling systems as well:

- the cassette operating system
- the disc operating system
- the network operating system

With the standard machines you will probably be using the cassette operating system. Within the cassette operating system, you can set various parameters:

*TAPE	Selects COS running at the default rate of 120 characters per second (1200 baud).
*TAPE 3	Selects COS running at the rate of 30 characters per second (300 baud).
*TAPE 12	Selects 1200 baud.

After you have keyed in your programs, you save the program on cassette for later reloading.

If you have one of the older operating systems, it is better to save the program twice, this will normally ensure that the program has been recorded correctly.

To save a program :

1. Key the program in.
2. Insert cassette into recorder.
3. Type SAVE "PROG", where PROG is the name of your program, then press <RETURN>.
4. A message then appears on the screen, RECORD then RETURN.
5. Press PLAY and RECORD on the tape and press RETURN

to let the computer know that you have done so.
6. If your cassette has MOTOR CONTROL then the tape
    will stop when the computer has finished recording
    your program. If MOTOR CONTROL is not present, you
    will have to stop the cassette yourself.
7. The prompt > will be displayed when the SAVE is
    complete

Once your program has been recorded successfully, you can
reload it at any time by using the following procedure:

1. Place cassette in recorder and wind to correct
    position on tape.
2. Type, LOAD "PROG" and press return.
3. The computer will present the message,
    Searching.
4. Press PLAY on your recorder.
5. When the computer finds your program it will
    display the message,
    Loading
6. The prompt > will be displayed when the LOAD is
    complete. You can then LIST or RUN your program as
    required.

Another command available under the COS is *CAT which will
CATalogue the contents of your tape.

The Printers

Some of the programs in this book require the use of a
printer, e.g the wordprocessor(P21) or the school
report(P101). Your model A machine will have to be upgraded
to enable it to drive a printer.

It is possible to do this job yourself, but it would be
better to see your supplier.

The Layout of The Book

That's enough technical data, let us return to the task in
hand, 100 programs for the BBC microcomputer.

Each program is laid out in the following format:

Program commentary.
Program listing.
Diagram of screen under execution, or printout where
appropriate.

Program Layout

There has been much ballyhoo about structured programming in
the computer press and there have been many attempts to
discredit the BASIC language.

The BBC dialect of BASIC is an attempt to overcome some of
the limitations of "traditional" BASIC.It is possible to
write fairly well laid out and well structured code in BBC
BASIC.

These programs represent an attempt to exploit these
features of BBC BASIC. However, the language does have its
limitations. You will occasionally find some rather long IF
statements, which can be difficult to read. This is due to a
lack of a multi-line IF statement, as is given in other
versions of BASIC such as COMAL.

It is possible to lay out programs using what is known as
LISTO formats, as used in the User Guide. I have not used
this feature of the BBC machine. I prefer to lay out code in
a manner that I find more natural.

When writing the programs, I first of all sketched out the
program using a pseudo form of BASIC, which was fairly well
structured. Thus when I came to code the programs, I already
knew the layout I required, so I did not use the layout
features of the machine.

The Machine Code Routine FNchar

In some of the programs, you will find a rather strange
looking routine, FNchar, which is used to inspect the screen
to find out what character is at the position being
inspected.

The routine is:

```
830 DEF FNchar(U,V)
840 PRINT TAB(U,V);
850 A%=135
860 =(USR(&FFF4) AND &FF00)/&100
```

Line 840 places the text cursor at position (u,v) on the
screen. Line 850 places the value 135 (86 hex) into the
accumulator. The routine called by USR(&FFF4) is one of the
OSBYTE calls documented in the User Guide page 432. ANDing
the integer returned from the USR call with &FF00, masks off
the least significant byte. Division by &100 leaves us with
the ASCII code for that character.

The User Guide states that this call is only implemented in
version 1.0. But I have been using it successfully on my own
machine, which was one of the first systems. To find out
which OS you have, use the call *FX0 which causes the
machine to print the OS, in my case, OS EPROM 0.01.

Keying In Your Programs

To help you to key in your programs take note of the
following points:

1. Use the AUTO feature, typically AUTO 100. This
    will automatically generate line numbers for you.
2. Use the fact that there is an automatic REPEAT on
    each key. If you have a lot of spaces to type in,
    just keep your finger on the space bar.
3. Use the cursor control and editing keys to keep
    the key press to a minimum.
4. To check your program listing, it is possible to
    put the BBC micro into page mode.
    Press the control key and N together, then LIST.
    The computer will only LIST a portion of the
    program. To get the next portion, press the SHIFT
    key. If you want to stop the listing press ESCAPE.
    To switch off page mode press the control key and
    the letter O together.
5. Use cursor control and copy keys to edit your
    programs.

Bugs

It is possible, of course, for things to go wrong, for bugs to be introduced into your code.

Part of the fun in programming is the finding and correcting of bugs. Indeed, correcting bugs often contributes to the process of introducing bugs.

Bugs can be introduced in various ways. I might have left a few bugs in the code. Hopefully, through the efforts of Prentice-Hall in carrying out field tests, these will be at a minimum.

Bugs can be introduced when you are keying in your programs. To catch these bugs you have to go through each section of the program in turn and try to locate it by eye and by testing the section. Using the page mode feature of the BBC micro can be very helpful at this stage.

Common errors are:

1. Using the letter O rather than the number 0.
2. Using the number one rather than the letter I.
3. Using lower case rather than the upper case.
4. Using the wrong dataname.
5. Going beyond the capabilities of the program.

Developing The Programs

In a sense, none of these programs are complete. They could all be expanded in various ways.

One of the joys of programming is to take a simple routine and give it a professional user friendly appearance. I have not attempted to make my programs complete in this sense. This is left up to you.

Do not feel shy about using the programs as routines within others. Consider this book to be a software library.

However, if you do use a routine within work of your own, I would be pleased if you were to acknowledge the source.

GO ON ENJOY YOUSELF.

P1 Nitemare

This program shows how dramatic effects can be produced
fairly easily with the BBC micro. The aim of the program is
to have a symmetric shape on the screen, changing colour
very quickly accompanied by a set of discordant noises –
hence the title.

The mode selected is 5, this allows us to have 4 colours on
the screen at any one time. Lines 190-220 select which 4
colours are chosen at any time. Eight radially symmetric
triangles are plotted on the screen followed by a random
discordant chord. Lines 330-350 (PROCtriangle) is used to
plot the triangles onto the screen.

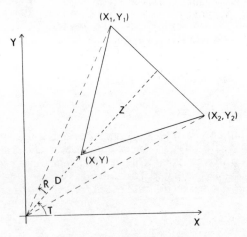

This procedure evaluates the coordinates of the corners of
the triangle as from the above figure.

COMMANDS

To play the program, simply key it in and type RUN.

```
100 REM Program P1 - Nitemare
110 MODE 5
120 REPEAT
130
140   R=RND(511)
150   T=RND(1)*PI*2
160   Z=RND(100)
170   D=RND(1)
180
190 REM change logical colours
200     FOR I%=0 TO 3
210       VDU 19,I%,RND(8)-1,0,0,0
220     NEXT I%
230
240 REM select actual colour
250     GCOL 0,RND(4)
260
270 REM draw 8 symmetric triangles
280     FOR I%=0 TO 7
290       PROCtriangle(R,T+PI/4*I%,Z)
300     NEXT I%
310
320 REM make random noise
330     FOR I%=1 TO 3
340       SOUND I%,-15,RND(64)*4-3,40
350     NEXT I%
360
370 UNTIL 0: REM do forever
380 END
390
400 DEF PROCtriangle(R,T,Z)
410
420       X=R*COS(T)+639
430       X1=(R+Z)*COS(T+D)+639
440       X2=(R+Z)*COS(T-D)+639
450       Y=R*SIN(T)+511
460       Y1=(R+Z)*SIN(T+D)+511
470       Y2=(R+Z)*SIN(T-D)+511
480
490       PLOT 4,X,Y
500       PLOT 4,X1,Y1
510       PLOT 85,X2,Y2
520 ENDPROC
```

P2 Musak

This program converts the BBC keyboard into a musical type keyboard. Lines 120-150 identify which keys are to be used. The numeric keys 1-9 select the duration of each note. VI$ selects those keys which are to be used to control channel-1, V2$ controls channel-2 and V3$ controls channel-3.

The sound is generated with "Flush Control" on, that is we use the command SOUND &ln,A,P,D in lines 220-240. This ensures that whenever a new note is selected the previous note is flushed from the channel queue and the sound is generated immediately.

There are two envelopes given in this example, try the effect of line 201 in the program. You will hear how the pitch is changed while the note is played - allowing for some interesting effects?

Note that when this program is running, the screen remains blank.

COMMANDS

To play the program, key in and then type RUN.
Use numeric key 0 to 9 to select duration of note.
Use keys "Q" to "P" to control channel 1.
Use keys "A" to "L" to control channel 2.
Use keys "Z" to "M" to control channel 3.

```
100 REM Program P2 - MUSAK
110 CLS
120 N$="123456789"
130 V1$="QWERTYUIOP"
140 V2$="ASDFGHJKL"
150 V3$="ZXCVBNM"
160 L=10
170 REPEAT
180     X$=GET$
190     X=INSTR(N$+V1$+V2$+V3$,X$)
200     IF X<10 THEN ENVELOPE 1,2*X,0,0,0,0,0,0,126,-10+X,0,
        -10+X,126,100-X*10
201 REM    IF X<10 THEN ENVELOPE 1,2*X,10,0,-10,100,100,100,
        126,-10+X,0,-10+X, 126,100-X*10
210     X=X-9
220     IF X>0 AND X<11 THEN SOUND &11,1,24+4*X,L
230     IF X>10 AND X<20 THEN SOUND &12,1,24+4*(X-10),L
240     IF X>19 AND X<28 THEN SOUND &13,1,24+4*(X-20),L
250 UNTIL 0
260 END
```

P3 Tunes

The BBC micro can be used to mimic the sound of many
instruments. In this program, we have almost a "bagpipe-ish"
sound. This is achieved by the 3 envelopes in lines 130-150.
Each envelope controls a seperate sound channel, and when
notes are played they are synchronised in lines 450-470.

The tune menu is placed on the screen in Mode 7, using
double-sized characters in different colours from normal.
This determines the form of the PRINT statements in lines
170-330.

The tunes are stored as data statements from line 1000
onwards. Notice how the correct tune is selected in line
400. The first two parameters allow you to change the speed
at which the tune is played and to change the pitch of the
tune.

Note that I have left some suspicious notes in tune number
three. I leave it as an exercise to the user to find the bad
notes.

Once you have found the bad notes you can alter the pitch to
correct them.

COMMANDS

Key in program and type RUN.
Press appropriate key from MENU.

```
100 REM Program P3 - Tunes
110
120
130 ENVELOPE 1,0,0,0,0,0,0,0,126,-4,0,-1,126,100
140 ENVELOPE 2,1,0,0,0,0,0,0,60,10,0,-60,60,120
150 ENVELOPE 3,30,0,0,0,0,0,0,100,-5,0,-5,100,10
160 MODE7
165 C$=CHR$(131)+CHR$(157)+CHR$(132)+CHR$(141)
170 PRINT C$"        T U N E S"
180 PRINT C$"        T U N E S"
190 PRINT C$
200 PRINT C$
210 PRINT C$"   1. Auld Lang Syne"
220 PRINT C$"   1. Auld Lang Syne"
230 PRINT C$"   2. Charlie is my Darling"
240 PRINT C$"   2. Charlie is my Darling"
250 PRINT C$"   3. Blow The Man Down"
```

```
260 PRINT C$"   3. Blow The Man Down"
270 PRINT C$
280 PRINT C$
290 PRINT C$"   4. end the program"
300 PRINT C$"   4. end the program"
310 PRINT CHR$(131);CHR$(157);CHR$(132)
320 PRINT CHR$(131);CHR$(157);CHR$(132)
330 PRINT CHR$(131);CHR$(157);CHR$(132)
340 REPEAT
350     PRINT TAB(0,18);C$;"Enter choice"
360     PRINT C$"Enter choice";CHR$(11);
370     choice=VAL(GET$)
380     PRINT CHR$(141);choice
390     PRINT CHR$(141);TAB(17,19);choice
400     IF choice<4 THEN RESTORE choice*1000 ELSE END
410     READ BEAT,ADJUST
420     REPEAT
430         READ P,D
440         D=D*BEAT:P=P+ADJUST
450         IF P=0 SOUND 1,0,0,D ELSE SOUND &201,3,P,D
460         IF P=0 SOUND 2,0,0,D ELSE SOUND &202,1,P-48,D
470         IF P=0 SOUND 3,0,0,D ELSE SOUND &203,2,P,D
480     UNTIL D=0
490 UNTIL 0
500 END

999 REM Auld Lang Syne
1000 DATA 1.75,0,101,4,121,6,121,2,121,4,137,4,129,6,121,2,
          129,4,137,4
1010 DATA 121,6,121,2,137,4,149,4,157,12,169,4,149,6,137,2,
          137,4,121,4
1020 DATA 129,6,121,2,129,4,137,2,129,2,121,6,109,2,109,4,
          101,4
1030 DATA 121,12,157,4,149,4,137,4,137,4,121,4,129,6,121,2,
          129,4,137,4
1040 DATA 149,2,137,6,137,4,149,4,157,12,169,4,149,6,137,2,
          137,4,121,4
1050 DATA 129,6,121,2,129,4,137,2,129,2,121,6,109,2,109,4,
          101,4,121,12
1060 DATA 0,0

1999 REM Charlie is my Darling
2000 DATA 1.3,0,109,6,117,2,121,6,129,2,137,8,157,6,165,2,
          169,8,165,6,157,8,137,8
2010 DATA 109,6,117,2,121,6,129,2,137,8,157,4,0,2,137,2,145,
          8,157,4,0,2,145,2,137,8,157,4,0,2,137,2
2020 DATA 109,6,129,2,121,6,129,2,137,8,157,6,165,2,169,8,
          165,6,157,2,157,12,157,4
```

```
2030 DATA 149,6,137,2,145,6,149,2,157,6,165,2,169,6,157,2,
          149,6,137,2,145,6,149,2,157,8,0,4,165,4
2040 DATA 169,6,165,2,169,6,157,2,149,4,137,4,121,4,129,2,
          137,2,145,6,129,2,137,6,121,2,117,8,121,6,117,2
2050 DATA 109,6,117,2,121,6,129,2,137,8,157,4,0,2,137,2,145,
          8,157,4,0,2,145,2,137,8,157,4,0,2,137,2
2060 DATA 109,6,117,2,121,6,129,2,137,8,157,4,0,2,165,2,
          169,8,165,6,157,2,157,12
2070 DATA 0,0


2999 REM Blow the Man Down
3000 DATA 2,-48,121,4,137,4,149,6,157,2,149,4,137,4,121,4,137,
          4,149,6,157,2,149,4,137,4,121,4,137,4
3010 DATA 149,6,157,6,145,6,137,2,145,4,129,8,137,4,145,6,137,
          2,145,4,129,4,117,4,101,4
3020 DATA 145,4,137,4,129,4,157,8,169,4,149,2,149,6,149,4,149,
          8,145,4,137,6,129,2
3030 DATA 137,4,121,4,0,0
```

P4 Pattern

This program generates patterns of straight lines reminiscent of "pin pictures". As it stands the program draws straight lines from points on two reference lines. It would be interesting to change this program to use curves rather than sraight lines.

The end points of the reference lines are given in lines 120 and 130, and the number of points per line in line 140. The equations of the lines in the form y=mx+c are calculated in 220-250, with the step sizes calculated in lines 200,210.

The program then simply steps down each line drawing straight lines to produce a pattern thus:

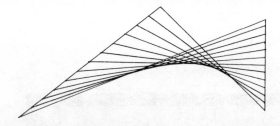

Note that as the program stands it cannot handle vertical lines, where the gradient calculation will give a division by zero error. This could of course be amended by the user.

COMMANDS

Key in program and type RUN.
Enter end points of lines when requested, followed by number of points per line.

```
100 REM Program P4 - Pattern
110 CLS
120 INPUT "What are the end points of line 1"'
          "(enter in the form X,Y)"X1,Y1,X2,Y2
130 INPUT "What are the end points of line 2"'
          "(enter in the form X,Y)"X3,Y3,X4,Y4
140 INPUT''"Enter the number of points per line"K
150 MODE 5: REM high res graphics
160 VDU 19,0,6;0;19,3,0;0;
170
180
190 REM The following section calculates the parameters
200 DX1=(X2-X1)/K
210 DX2=(X4-X3)/K
220 M1=(Y2-Y1)/(X2-X1)
230 M2=(Y4-Y3)/(X4-X3)
240 B1=Y1-M1*X1
250 B2=Y3-M2*X3
260 MOVE X1,Y1:DRAW X2,Y2
270 MOVE X3,Y3:DRAW X4,Y4
280 FOR I=1 TO K
290    MOVE X1+I*DX1,M1*(X1+I*DX1)+B1
300    GCOL 3,I
310    DRAW X4-I*DX2,M2*(X4-I*DX2)+B2
320 NEXT I
330 END
```

P5 Graph Plotting

A slightly mathematical program here – it is used to plot the graph of a mathematical function. In most micros this would have been an awkward program to write, but BBC BASIC provides us with the EVAL function, which allows us to input the function as a simple string and then EVALuate the function at each point to be plotted.

This program also illustrates the use of normal characters to build up a LOGO on the screen. To help you in coding such a screen use a "text planning sheet" as given in the User Guide. Lines 170–300 show what kind of effect can be achieved with the BBC micro.

Lines 350–440 set up the parameters for the function to be plotted. Notice that there has been an attempt to trap errors at this point by using the flag "K".

Lines 460–670 draw and label the axes, with the function being plotted lines 690–740.

Notice that the labelling of the axes is achieved by joining the text and graphics cursors (line 610).

COMMANDS

Key in program and type RUN.
Enter function of X when requested. If Y-range is not specified it is given as –512 to 512.
Note that X must be in upper case, and that only the right hand side of f(X) is entered.


```
100 REM Program P5 - Graph Plot
110 MODE 4
120 REM change colours
130 VDU 19,0,4,0,0,0
140 VDU 19,1,3,0,0,0
150
```

```
160 REM display logo
170 PRINT''''
180 PRINT"    ##    ####      #     ####   #    #"
190 PRINT"   #  #   #    #    # #    #    # #   #"
200 PRINT"   #          #   #   #   #    #  # #   #"
210 PRINT"   #   ###  ####    #####   ####   ####"
220 PRINT"   #    #   #    #  #    #     #  #      #   #"
230 PRINT"   ####   #    # #   # #      #    #   #"
240 PRINT''''
250 PRINT"        ####  #       ####  #####"
260 PRINT"        #    # #  #     #     #    #"
270 PRINT"        #    # #  #     #     #    #"
280 PRINT"        ####  #       #     #    #"
290 PRINT"        #       #       #     #    #"
300 PRINT"        #      #####  ####    #"
310
320 wait$=INKEY$(200)
330 CLS
340 INPUT ''''"Function to be plotted",function$
350 REPEAT
360   K=1
370   INPUT "Max X value ",XMAX
380   INPUT "Min X value ",XMIN
390   IF XMIN>XMAX THEN PRINT "XMIN >XMAX":K=0
400   INPUT "Do you wish to specify Y_range"ANS$
410   YMIN=-512:YMAX=512
420   IF LEFT$(ANS$,1)="Y" THEN
      INPUT '"Ymax ",YMAX:INPUT "Ymin ",YMIN
430   IF YMIN>YMAX THEN PRINT "YMIN>YMAX":K=0
440 UNTIL K=1
450
460 REM draw axes
470 CLS
480 XRANGE=XMAX-XMIN
490 YRANGE=YMAX-YMIN
500 DX=XRANGE/1280
510 DY=YRANGE/1024
520
530 REM CX,CY coords of centre
540 IF YMIN<0 THEN CY=ABS(YMIN) ELSE CY=0
550 CY=CY/DY
560 MOVE 0,CY:DRAW 1280,CY
570 IF XMIN<0 THEN CX=ABS(XMIN) ELSE CX=0
580 CX=CX/DX
590 MOVE CX,0:DRAW CX,1024
600
```

```
610 VDU 5:REM join text and graphics cursor
620 FOR I=0 TO 7
630   MOVE 160*I,CY
640   PRINT STR$(INT(((160*I*DX)+XMIN)*10+.5)/10)
650   MOVE CX+4,128*I
660   PRINT STR$(INT(((128*I*DY)+YMIN)*10+.5)/10)
670 NEXT I
680
690 GCOL 4,1
700 FOR I=0 TO 1280 STEP 4
710   X=XMIN+I*DX
720   Y=(EVAL(function$)-YMIN)/DY
730   PLOT 69,I,Y
740 NEXT I
750
760 VDU 4:REM separate cursors
770 PRINT "Plot of Y="function$
780 END
```

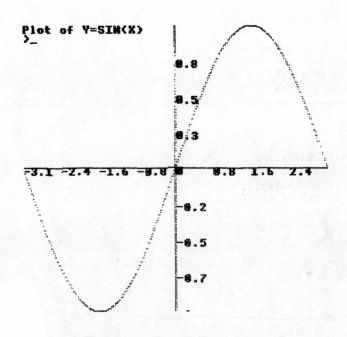

P6 Bouncing Ball 1

This program shows a simple method of achieving animation, in normal text mode. The mode selected is the teletext mode 7, which has some graphics features, but these are not used in this program. The "ball" is the letter o.

Animation is accomplished by placing the ball on the screen and then placing a space character on top; the ball is then printed one position on.

Take out line 160 to see the effect of the flashing cursor which tends to annoy the viewer. (If you have version 1.0 of the operating system use line 170 without the first REM instead of 160).

COMMANDS

Key in program and RUN.

```
100 REM Program P6 - Bouncing Ball 1
110 MODE7
120 X=RND(30)+2
130 Y=RND(18)+2
140 DX=1
150 DY=1
160 VDU 23;8202;0;0 :REM Switch cursor off
170 REM VDU 23,1,0;0;0;0 : REM vers 1.0 OS
180 PRINT TAB(X,Y);
190 REPEAT
200    PRINT TAB(X,Y);"o";
210    IF X=2 OR X=36 THEN DX=-DX
220    IF Y=2 OR Y=22 THEN DY=-DY
230    FOR I=1 TO 15:NEXT I
240    PRINT TAB(X,Y);" ";
250    X=X+DX
260    Y=Y+DY
270 UNTIL 0
```

P7 Bouncing Ball 2

This program should be compared with program 6, in that they both give a similar result - a shape bouncing around the screen. However, in graphics mode it is simpler to draw other shapes onto the screen - e.g. the box around the ball.

Change the conditions in lines 250,260 to see the effect of bursting a hole in the wall. Other effects which can be experimented with are to draw a snake instead of a ball in lines 210-240, or not to unplot the ball in lines 270-300.

Colour has not been implemented in this program, but four are available. What about three different coloured balls bouncing around the screen?

COMMANDS

Key in program and type RUN.

```
100 REM Program P7 - Bouncing Ball 2
110 MODE5
120 VDU 5
130 MOVE 10,10
140 DRAW 10,1000
150 DRAW 1000,1000
160 DRAW 1000,10
170 DRAW 10,10
180 X%=RND(800)+100:Y%=RND(800)+100
190 DX%=10:DY%=20
200 REPEAT
210    PLOT 69,X%,Y%
220    PLOT 69,X%,Y%+1
230    PLOT 69,X%+1,Y%
240    PLOT 69,X%+1,Y%+1
250    IF (X%+DX%)>999 OR (X%+DX%)<13 THEN DX%=-DX%
260    IF (Y%+DY%)>999 OR (Y%+DY%)<13 THEN DY%=-DY%
270    PLOT 71,X%,Y%
280    PLOT 71,X%,Y%+1
290    PLOT 71,X%+1,Y%
300    PLOT 71,X%+1,Y%+1
310    X%=X%+DX%:Y%=Y%+DY%
320 UNTIL 0
330
340 END
```

P8 Jimmy

This is another animation program except that this time we are using the user defined characters to create a cartoon figure, Jimmy.

As an example of the use of Jimmy, lines 190-350 wave his left hand.

To change one of the user defined characters use a user defined character planning sheet as shown in the User Guide.

It is left to the user to build up the full Jimmy character set. There are seventeen characters available.

COMMANDS

Key in program and RUN.
Key in your own routines between lines 160 and 360, and see how to make Jimmy move.

```
100 REM Program P8 - Jimmy
110 DIM JIMMY$(31)
120 MODE5
130 FOR I=224 TO 255
140    READ B1%,B2%,B3%,B4%,B5%,B6%,B7%,B8%
150    VDU 23,I,B1%,B2%,B3%,B4%,B5%,B6%,B7%,B8%
160    JIMMY$(I-224)=CHR$(I)
170 NEXT I
180
190 REM We can now play with Jimmy,
        the following code waves his left hand
200
210 PRINT TAB(9,8) JIMMY$(0)
220 PRINT TAB(8,9) JIMMY$(8);JIMMY$(2)
230 PRINT TAB(8,10) JIMMY$(9);JIMMY$(3)
240 PRINT TAB(8,11) JIMMY$(18);JIMMY$(16);JIMMY$(17)
250
```

```
260 REPEAT
270    PRINT TAB(10,9) JIMMY$(6)
280    PRINT TAB(10,10) JIMMY$(7)
290    FOR I=1 TO 300:NEXT I
300    PRINT TAB(10,10) " "
310    PRINT TAB(10,9) JIMMY$(13)
320    PRINT TAB(10,8) JIMMY$(12)
330    FOR I=1 TO 300:NEXT I
340    PRINT TAB(10,8) " "
350 UNTIL 0
360 END
370
380 DATA 24,60,90,126,126,102,62,24:REM HEAD ON
390 DATA 0,0,0,0,0,0,0,0:REM HEAD PROFILE
400 DATA 24,255,255,255,231,126,102,126:REM UPPER TRUNK ON
410 DATA 102,60,60,60,126,231,231,231:REM LOWER TRUNK ON
420 DATA 0,0,0,0,0,0,0,0
430 DATA 0,0,0,0,0,0,0,0
440 DATA 0,128,192,224,112,48,48,48:REM UPPER LEFT ARM
450 DATA 48,48,48,0,0,0,0,0:REM LOWER LEFT ARM
460 DATA 0,1,3,7,14,12,12,12:REM UPPER RIGHT ARM
470 DATA 12,12,12,0,0,0,0,0:REM LOWER RIGHT ARM
480 DATA 0,0,0,0,0,0,0,0
490 DATA 0,0,0,0,0,0,0,0
500 DATA 0,0,0,48,48,48,48,48:REM UPPER RAISE LEFT
510 DATA 112,240,192,128,0,0,0,0:REM LOWER RAISE LEFT
520 DATA 0,0,0,0,0,0,0,0
530 DATA 0,0,0,0,0,0,0,0
540 DATA 231,231,231,231,231,231,231,231:REM LEGS ATTENTION
550 DATA 0,0,0,0,0,0,192,192:REM LEFT FOOT
560 DATA 0,0,0,0,0,0,3,3:REM RIGHT FOOT
570 DATA 0,0,0,0,0,0,0,0
580 DATA 0,0,0,0,0,0,0,0
590 DATA 0,0,0,0,0,0,0,0
600 DATA 0,0,036,60,60,255,255:REM HAT
610 DATA 0,24,60,126,126,60,24,0:REM BALL
620 DATA 60,126,255,126,60,24,24,24:REM BAT
630 DATA 0,0,0,0,0,0,0,0
640 DATA 0,0,0,0,0,0,0,0
650 DATA 0,0,0,0,0,0,0,0
660 DATA 0,0,0,0,0,0,0,0
670 DATA 0,0,0,0,0,0,0,0
680 DATA 0,0,0,0,0,0,0,0
690 DATA 0,0,0,0,0,0,0,0
700 DATA 0,0,0,0,0,0,0,0
710 REM end of program
```

P9 Clock

This program uses graphics, sound and text to produce a
simple analogue clock on the screen.

COMMANDS

Key in program and type RUN.
Set clock when requested.

```
100 REM Program P9 - Clock
110
120 REM Initialise time
130 MODE 7
140 PRINT ''"Enter the time as prompted"
150 INPUT''"What is the hour?",H
160 INPUT ''"What is the minute?",M
170 INPUT ''"What is the second?",S
180 TIME=0
190
200 REM Draw face and set colours
210 MODE 5
220 VDU 19,0,5;0;
230 R=400:A=0
240
250 REM Draw clock
260 GCOL 0,2
270 MOVE 0,0:MOVE 639,511:PLOT 85,1240,0
280 MOVE R+639,511
290 GCOL 0,1
300 REPEAT
310     MOVE 639,511
320     PLOT 85,R*COS(A)+639,R*SIN(A)+511
330     A=A+.1
340     PLOT 85,R*COS(A)+639,R*SIN(A)+511
350     A=A+.1
360 UNTIL A>2*PI+.01
370
380 REM Plot hour markers
390 GCOL 0,0
400 FOR I=1 TO 12
410     P1=350*COS(RAD(30*I))+639
420     P2=350*SIN(RAD(30*I))+511
430     Q1=380*COS(RAD(30*I))+639
440     Q2=380*SIN(RAD(30*I))+511
450     MOVEP1,P2:DRAW Q1;Q2
```

```
460 NEXT I
470
480 REM set tick
490 ENVELOPE 1,1,0,0,0,0,0,0,100,-100,0,-100,126,0
500 SOUND 1,0,255,-1
510
520 REM Adjust time settings
530 S=S+(TIME DIV 100) MOD 60
540 M=M+(TIME DIV 6000)MOD 60
550 H=H+(TIME DIV 360000) MOD 12
560
570 REM Scale for clock: -46 is 12 o'clock
580 H=(92-30*H-M/2)*2
590 M=-46-M
600 S=-46-S
610
620
630 REM Sweep second hand
640 VDU 29,639;511;
650 M=M+1
660 PROCminute
670 REPEAT
680    TIME=0
690    GCOL 0,1
700    X=COS(RAD(6*(S+1))):Y=SIN(RAD(6*(S+1)))
710    MOVE 300*X,300*Y
720    DRAW 340*X,340*Y
730    GCOL 0,3
740    SOUND &10,1,3,10
750    X=COS(RAD(6*S)):Y=SIN(RAD(6*S))
760    MOVE 300*X,300*Y
770    DRAW 340*X,340*Y
780    S=(S-1) MOD 60
790    IF S=-57 THEN PROCminute
800 PROCwait
810 UNTIL 0
820 END
830
840 DEF PROCminute
850 GCOL 0,1
860 MOVE 0,0
870 DRAW 300*COS(RAD(6*(M+1))),300*SIN(RAD(6*(M+1)))
880 MOVE 0,0
890 GCOL 0,3
900 DRAW 300*COS(RAD(6*M)),300*SIN(RAD(6*M))
910 M=(M-1) MOD 60
920 GCOL 0,1
```

```
 930 MOVE 0,0
 940 DRAW 200*COS(RAD((H+1)/2)),200*SIN(RAD((H+1)/2))
 950 MOVE 0,0
 960 GCOL 0,3
 970 DRAW 200*COS(RAD(H/2)),200*SIN(RAD(H/2))
 980 H=(H-1) MOD 720
 990 ENDPROC
1000
1010 DEF PROCwait
1020 REPEAT:UNTIL TIME=100
1030 ENDPROC
```

P10 Soft Keys - Program Development

This is a program I have found very useful in program development. The program first of all writes a set of commands at the bottom of the screen and then programs the Soft Keys corresponding to these commands. A text window is then defined which makes sure that the Soft Key line is not erased except when changing modes.

Instead of using a line of text on the screen it can be useful to write the Soft Key commands on a piece of paper and slip it under the plastic strip above the Soft Keys.

COMMANDS

Key in program and type RUN.
Press Soft Key 7 to start.


```
100 REM Program P10 - Soft Keys
110 CLS
120 PRINT TAB(5,15)" Program development system"
130 X=INKEY(100)
140 CLS
150 PRINT TAB(0,24)"AUTO  REN. REM DATA DEL. MODE7 CLS GO";
160 *KEY0"AUTO"
170 *KEY1"REN."
180 *KEY2"REM"
190 *KEY3"DATA"
200 *KEY4"DEL."
210 *KEY5"MODE7"
220 *KEY6"CLS"
230 *KEY7"NEW|MCLS|M"
240 VDU 28,0,23,39,0
250 VDU 30
```

P11   Mastermind

This program implements the first version of the popular
game by INVICTA, Ltd.

The object of the game is to determine the colour of the
four squares on the screen, the user has up to twenty
attempts at working out the code.

When you enter an attempt, the computer responds by
indicating whether you have a coloured square in the correct
position, or whether you have a correctly coloured square,
but it is in the wrong position.

For each correct square in the correct position, the
computer places a magenta dash to the right of the guess.

For each correct square in the wrong position the computer
places a cyan (light blue) dash to the right of the guess.

COMMANDS

Key in program and type RUN.
Enter guess as e.g. RGYB.

```
100 REM Program P11 - Mastermind
110 MODE7
120 DIM colour(3),guess(3),temp(3)
130 FOR I=0 TO 22
140    PRINT CHR$(135);CHR$(157)
150 NEXT I
160 PRINT TAB(12,0) CHR$(149);"|  |  |  |"
170 line=0
180 FOR I=0 TO 3
190    colour(I)=RND(4)+144
200 temp(I)=colour(I)
210 NEXT I
220 REPEAT
230    line=line+1
240    FOR I= 0 TO 3
250       colour(I)=temp(I)
260    NEXT I
270    PRINT TAB(3,23);
280 REM Program will be unsatisfactory if more than
          4 characters are input
```

```
290    INPUT "Enter colour pattern eg: RGYB " patt$
300    PRINT TAB(3,23) STRING$(40," ");
310    FOR I= 0 TO 3
320      guess(I)=149
330      IF MID$(patt$,I+1,1)="R" THEN guess(I)=145
340      IF MID$(patt$,I+1,1)="G" THEN guess(I)=146
350      IF MID$(patt$,I+1,1)="Y" THEN guess(I)=147
360      IF MID$(patt$,I+1,1)="B" THEN guess(I)=148
370      PRINT TAB(12+I*3,line) CHR$(guess(I));"|";
380    NEXT I
390    pc=0:cc=0
400    FOR I=0 TO 3
410     IF guess(I)=colour(I) THEN pc=pc+1:colour(I)=0:guess(I)=1
420    NEXT I
430    FOR I=0 TO 3
440      FOR J=0 TO 3
450       IF guess(I)=colour(J) THEN cc=cc+1:colour(J)=0:J=3
460      NEXT J
470    NEXT I
480    IF pc>0 THEN PROCposn
490    IF cc>0 THEN PROCcolour
500 UNTIL pc=4 OR line=20
510 IF pc=4 CLS:PRINT TAB(12,12) "W E L L    D O N E !!",
                 TAB( 12,14);"YOU TOOK "line" ATTEMPTS" :END
520 CLS
530 PRINT '''''"THE CORRECT CODE WAS"
540 FOR I=0 TO 3
550    PRINT TAB(12+I*3,12) CHR$(temp(I));"|";
560 NEXT I
570 PRINT
580 END
590
600 DEF PROCposn
610 FOR I=1 TO pc
620    PRINT TAB(25+I*2,line) CHR$(149);CHR$(172);
630 NEXT I
640 ENDPROC
650
660 DEF PROCcolour
670 FOR I=1 TO cc
680    PRINT TAB(25+pc*2+ I*2,line) CHR$(150);CHR$(172);
690 NEXT I
700 ENDPROC
```

P12   Guess the Number

In this simple game the user has to try to outguess the
computer. The computer selects a random whole number between
1 and 100, and the user has to find it out.

The instructions for this program are included within the
code.

COMMANDS

Key in program and type RUN.
Follow instructions.

```
100 REM Program P12 - Guess the Number
110 MODE 7
120 PRINT TAB(12,12)CHR$(141);CHR$(132);"GUESS THE NUMBER "
130 PRINT TAB(12,13)CHR$(141);CHR$(131);"GUESS THE NUMBER "
140 Z=INKEY(300)
150 CLS
160
170 PRINT '''CHR$(130);"In this program you attempt to "
180 PRINT CHR$(130);"outguess the computer. You will be"
190 PRINT CHR$(130);"prompted to guess a number between"
200 PRINT CHR$(130);"0 and 100. If you guess wrongly"
210 PRINT CHR$(130);"the computer will tell you if you are"
220 PRINT CHR$(130);"too low or too high. When finished"
230 PRINT CHR$(130);"the computer will give you your"
240 PRINT CHR$(130);"average number of attempts to "
250 PRINT CHR$(129);"GUESS THE NUMBER"
260 PRINT '''CHR$(130);"Press any key to start"
270 Z=GET
280
290 CLS
300 goes=0
310 attempts=0
320
330 REPEAT
340    goes=goes+1
350    number=RND(TIME) MOD 100
360    correct=0
370
```

PFBM-B*

```
380    REPEAT
390      PRINT TAB(0,12);CHR$(133);"Enter your guess   ";
400      INPUT guess
410      CLS
420      IF guess<number THEN
         PRINT TAB(0,12);CHR$(129);"Too low"
430      IF guess>number THEN
         PRINT TAB(0,12);CHR$(134);"Too high"
440      IF guess=number THEN
         PRINT TAB(0,12);CHR$(136);CHR$(131);"Correct":
         correct=-1
450      Z=INKEY(300)
460      attempts=attempts+1
470    UNTIL correct
480
490    CLS
500    PRINT TAB(0,12);CHR$(133);"Another go (Y/N)";
510    INPUT a$
520  UNTIL a$<>"y" AND a$<>"Y"
530
540  CLS
550  average=attempts/goes
560  PRINT TAB(0,12);CHR$(133);
     "You took an average of "average" per shot"
570  IF average<7 THEN
     PRINT TAB(0,15);CHR$(133);"P R E T T Y  G O O D "
580  END
```

P13 Reaction Test

This program could help your keyboard skills. The computer places a random character on the screen and starts to time your response.

The object of the game is to press the required key as fast as possible.

When the program is complete an average reaction time is displayed on the screen.

COMMANDS

Key in program and type RUN.

```
100 REM Program P13 - Reaction Test
110 MODE 7
120 PRINT TAB(12,12)"REACTION TEST"
130 Z=INKEY(300)
140 CLS
150 PRINT TAB(0,12)"How many tries do you want?";
160 INPUT no_of_attempts
170 PRINT "Press any key to start":Z=GET
180 FOR letter=1 TO no_of_attempts
190    CLS
200    TIME=0
210    X=RND(39):Y=RND(24)
220    A$=CHR$(RND(25)+65)
230    PRINT TAB(X,Y) A$
240     REPEAT
250        B$=GET$
260     UNTIL B$=A$
270    tot_time=tot_time+TIME
280 NEXT letter
290
300 CLS
310 PRINT TAB(0,10)"Number of attempts "no_of_attempts
320 PRINT "Total time ";tot_time/100" seconds"
330 PRINT "Average reaction time was ";
        tot_time/no_of_attempts/100;" seconds"
340 END
```

P14 Gobble

In this program we show the effects of simple graphics.

We have two beasties eating up a field of grass. This is a two-player game, with each player taking the part of one of the beasties.

```
                          W
Player 1  uses keys      A    S
                          Z


                          @
Player 2  uses keys      ;    :
                          /
```

Player 1 moves up and down using keys W and Z
         moves left and right using   A and S.

Player 2 moves up and down using keys @ and /
         moves left and right using   ; and :.

If a player leaves the field or attempts to eat a patch of grass which has already been eaten, he dies.

Every time a piece is eaten points are scored.

COMMANDS

Key in program and type RUN.
Use keys as described above.

```
100 REM Program P14 - Gobble
110
120 REM Set up board
130 MODE 5
140 VDU 19,0,2;0;
150 VDU 23;8202;0;0;0
160 GCOL 0,3
170 MOVE 0,0
180 DRAW 1279,0
```

```
190 DRAW 1279,1023
200 DRAW 0,1023
210 DRAW 0,0
220
230 REM Initialise parameters
240 DIM X(2),Y(2),DX(2),DY(2),score(2)
250 X(1)=16:X(2)=1263:Y(1)=512:Y(2)=512
260 PLOT 69,8,512:PLOT 69,1271,512
270 A=1:B=2
280 gameover=FALSE
290 flag=0
300
310 REM Play game
320 REPEAT
330   DX(1)=(INKEY(-66)-INKEY(-82))*8
340   DX(2)=(INKEY(-88)-INKEY(-73))*8
350   DY(1)=(INKEY(-98)-INKEY(-34))*4
360   DY(2)=(INKEY(-105)-INKEY(-72))*4
370   FOR I=A TO B
380     IF DX(I)+DY(I)=0 THEN VDU 0 ELSE
             IF POINT(X(I)+DX(I),Y(I)+DY(I))<>0
             THEN PROCbang(I) ELSE PROCmove(I)
390   NEXT I
400 UNTIL gameover
410
420 REM Display result
430 MODE7
440 PRINT TAB(0,12);CHR$(141);"Player 1's score is ";
          CHR$(136);score(1);
450 PRINT TAB(0,13);CHR$(141) "Player 1's score is ";
          CHR$(136);score(1);
460 PRINT TAB(0,16);CHR$(141) "Player 2's score is ";
          CHR$(136);score(2);
470 PRINT TAB(0,17);CHR$(141);"Player 2's score is ";
          CHR$(136);score(2)
480   PRINT
490 *FX15,0
500 END
510
520
530 DEF PROCbang(i)
540   SOUND 0,-15,53,4
550   IF i=1 THEN A=2 ELSE B=1
560   flag=flag+1
570   IF flag=2 THEN gameover=TRUE
580 ENDPROC
590
```

```
600
610 DEF PROCmove(i)
620   X(i)=X(i)+DX(i)
630   Y(i)=Y(i)+DY(i)
640   PLOT 69,X(i),Y(i)
650   score(i)=score(i)+1
660 ENDPROC
```

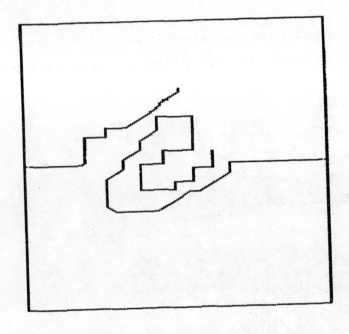

P15   Tennis

This is an adaptation of an old video game. We have two
players playing tennis on a green pitch.

Player 1 uses keys Z and X to move his bat up and down.
Player 2 uses keys . and / to move his bat up and down.

The score is displayed at the top of the screen. There are a
total of fifty balls available in the game, rather more than
in the old video games.

This is an interesting program in that no graphics are used.
All movements are accomplished by print statements.

Try using *FX11 and *FX12 commands to improve the program.

COMMANDS

Key in program and type RUN.

        Player 1 uses Z for up,
                      X for down.

        Player 2 uses / for up,
                      . for down.

```
100 REM Program P15 - Tennis
110 MODE4
120 @%=2
130 balls_left=50
140 DIM goals(2)
150 VDU 19,0,2;0;19,7,0;0;
160 VDU 23,224,24,90,90,255,255,90,90,24
170 VDU 23,225,24,24,24,24,24,24,24,24
180 VDU 23;8202;0;0;0;
190 ball$=CHR$(224)
200 unball$=" "
210 bat$=CHR$(225)+CHR$(10)+CHR$(8)+CHR$(225)+
        CHR$(10)+CHR$(8)+CHR$(225)
220 unbat$=" "+CHR$(10)+CHR$(8)+" "+CHR$(10)+CHR$(8)+" "
230 PRINT TAB(0,16);bat$;TAB(39,16);bat$;
240 player_1=16:player_2=16
250 X%=19:Y%=RND(27)+1
260 IF RND(4)>2 THEN DX%=-1 ELSE DX%=1
270 IF RND(4)>2 THEN DY%=-1 ELSE DY%=1
```

```
280 REPEAT
290   PRINT TAB(X%,Y%)unball$;
300   X%=X%+DX%:Y%=Y%+DY%
310   IF Y%<2 OR Y%>29 THEN PROCwall_bounce
320   PRINT TAB(X%,Y%) ball$;
330   PROCbat
340 UNTIL balls_left=0
350
360 PRINT "Finished, give me more money!!!"
370 REPEAT : UNTIL INKEY$(100)="Q"
380 END
390
400 DEF PROCwall_bounce
410     SOUND &11,-15,100,2
420     DY%=-DY%
430 ENDPROC
440
450 DEF PROCbat
460   key$=INKEY$(2)
470   D_player_1=(key$=CHR$(90))*-4+(key$=CHR$(88))*4
480   D_player_2=(key$=CHR$(46))*-4+(key$=CHR$(47))*4
490   temp_1=player_1+D_player_1
500   temp_2=player_2+D_player_2
510   IF temp_1<29 AND temp_1>-1 THEN PRINT TAB(0,player_1)
      unbat$;:PRINT TAB(0,temp_1) bat$;:player_1=temp_1
520   IF temp_2<29 AND temp_2>-1 THEN PRINT TAB(39,player_2)
      unbat$;:PRINT TAB(39,temp_2) bat$;:player_2=temp_2
530   IF X%=39 AND ABS(Y%-player_2-1)<2 THEN SOUND &11,-15,100,2:
      DX%=-DX% ELSE IF X%=39 PROCscore(1)
540   IF X%=0 AND ABS(Y%-player_1-1)<2 THEN SOUND &11,-15,100,2:
      DX%=-DX% ELSE IF X%=0 PROCscore(2)
550 ENDPROC
560
570 DEF PROCscore(k)
580   SOUND &11,-15,64,4
590   balls_left=balls_left-1
600   goals(k)=goals(k)+1
610   PRINT TAB(k*10,0) goals(k);
620   PRINT TAB(X%,Y%) unball$;
630   X%=19
640 FOR I=1 TO 20:PROCbat:NEXT I
650 ENDPROC
```

P16   Bombs

In this program, the user has to defend his city against attacks from the sky.

The game is played purely in text, with many user defined characters. The city is built up in lines 230 to 360.

The user has control of a laser gun which can be used to knock out bombs which appear at random at the top of the screen.

To control the gun we use the edit keys (hence the use of *FX4,1) to move horizontally and <COPY> to fire the gun.

The game finishes when the city is destroyed, which can take some time!

If you find the COPY key too awkward to use then change line 480 to look for the space bar, thus:

        480   IF K=32 AND FLAG=0 THEN PROCfire

If you find that the edit keys no longer work after playing this game, then use *FX4,0 to fix it.

COMMANDS

Key in program and type RUN.
Use cursor control keys to move gun.
Press <COPY> key to fire.

Bombs blasted   Bombs landed   3
                                        Y

```
100 REM Program P16 - Bombs
110 FLAG=0:F=0
120 @%=&3
130 MODE4
140 VDU 19,0,5;0;19,3,7;0;
150 REM Define characters
160 VDU 23,224,255,153,153,255,255,129,129,255
170 VDU 23,225,24,126,231,219,219,231,126,0
180 VDU 23,226,231,102,60,24,24,24,24,24
190 VDU 23,227,0,0,0,24,24,0,0,0
200 SHELL$=CHR$(227)
210 BOMB$=CHR$(226)
220 D$=CHR$(225)
230 C$=CHR$(224)
240 C2$=C$+C$
250 C3$=C2$+C$
260 C7$=C3$+C2$+C2$
270 C10$=C7$+C3$
280 C16$=C7$+C7$+C2$
290 C18$=C16$+C2$
300 PRINT TAB(4,24)C3$+"      "+C2$+"    "+
        C3$+"    "+C3$+"       "+C3$
310 PRINT"     "+C3$+"      "+C2$+"   "+C3$+"       "+
        C3$+"      "+C3$+"     "+C3$
320 PRINT"      "+C3$+" "+C10$+"     "+C16$
330 PRINTC7$+" "+C10$+"     "+C18$
340 PRINTC7$+" "+C10$+"      "+C18$
350 PRINT"      "+C3$+" "+C10$+"      "+C18$
360 PRINT"       "+C3$+" "+C10$+"      "+C18$
370 A=20
380 *FX4,1
390 B%=RND(38)
400 Z%=1
410 MOVE 0,0
420 PRINTTAB(20,0)"Bombs landed ";:HIT%=0
430 PRINT TAB(0,0)"Bombs blasted";:Blast%=0
440 R%=A:S%=23
450 REPEAT
460    PRINT TAB(35,0)HIT%;
470    K=ASC(INKEY$(0))
480    IF K=135 AND FLAG=0 THEN PROCfire
490    IF FLAG=1 THEN PRINT TAB(R%,S%-1)SHELL$;:
       PRINT TAB(R%,S%)" ";:PROCbang:S%=S%-1
500    K=(K=136)-(K=137)+(A=39)-(A=0)
510    PRINT TAB(A,23)" ";
520    PRINT TAB(A+K,23)D$;
530    A=A+K
```

```
540    G=1280*((B%)/40)+16:H=1023*((30.5-Z%)/32)
550    Q=(POINT(G,H)=1)
560    IF F=1 THEN PRINT TAB(B%,Z%)" ";:
       PRINT TAB(B%,Z%+1)BOMB$;:Z%=Z%+1
570    F=(F+1) MOD 3
580    IF Z%=30 OR Q THEN PRINT TAB(B%,Z%)" "+
       CHR$(8)+CHR$(10)+" ";:Z%=1:B%=RND(38):
       HIT%=HIT%+1
590 UNTIL HIT%=555
600 END
610
620 DEF PROCfire
630    FLAG=1
640    R%=A
650    SOUND0,-15,67,2
660 ENDPROC
670
680 DEF PROCbang
690    T=(B%=R%) AND ((S%=Z%+1) OR (S%=Z%+2))
700    IF T THEN SOUND 1,-15,53,2:Blast%=Blast%+1:
       PRINT TAB(14,0)Blast%:Z%=1:B%=RND(38)
710    IF T OR S%=3 THEN FLAG=0:
       PRINT TAB(R%,S%-1)" "+CHR$(8)+CHR$(11)+" ":R%=A:S%=23
720 ENDPROC
```

P17   Bat'n'Moths   MODEL B ONLY

This was my first game on the BEEB. The game developed from
an idea of my wife's, who designed the various characters
used in the game.

The object of the game is to control a bat to attempt to eat
a set of moths which flit about on the screen.

This can be a fairly difficult game, so there is a parameter
'D' which is used to slow down the moths. D can hold any
value between 0 and 5, 4 being difficult.

As in P16, we use the cursor control key to move the bat and
COPY to gobble the moths. All four cursor keys are used to
move the bat.

COMMAND

Key in program and type RUN.
Use cursor control keys to move bat.
Press <COPY> key to eat moth.

```
100 REM Program P17 -Bat'n'Moths
110 DIM X%(10),Y%(10)
120 DIM DX%(10),DY%(10)
130 MODE4
140 REM VDU 23,1,0;0;0;0;
150 VDU 23;8202;0;0;0;
160 FOR I=224 TO 229
170   READ B1,B2,B3,B4,B5,B6,B7,B8
180   VDU 23,I,B1,B2,B3,B4,B5,B6,B7,B8
190 NEXT I
200 REM define characters
210 M1$=CHR$(224):M2$=CHR$(225)
220 BAT$=CHR$(226)+CHR$(227)+CHR$(8)+CHR$(8)+
        CHR$(10)+CHR$(228)+CHR$(229)
230 UNBAT$=" "+CHR$(8)+CHR$(8)+CHR$(10)+"  "
240 REM change colours
250 VDU 19,0,4,0,0,0
260 VDU 19,1,3,0,0,0
270 INPUT "Number of moths (1 to 10) ",K:K=K-1
280 FOR I%=0 TO K:X%(I%)=RND(39):
    Y%(I%)=RND(31):NEXT I%
290 *FX4,1
300 INPUT "Difficulty (0 to 5)",D:D=5-D
310 CLS
320 BX=20:BY=16
330 PRINT TAB(BX,BY)BAT$;
340 FOR I%=0 TO K
350   DX%(I%)=1:DY%(I%)=1
360 NEXT I%
370 REPEAT
380   FOR I%=0 TO K
390     IF (X%(I%)+DX%(I%))>38 OR (X%(I%)+DX%(I%))<1
        THEN DX%(I%)=-DX%(I%)*2
400     IF (Y%(I%)+DY%(I%))>30 OR (Y%(I%)+DY%(I%))<1
        THEN DY%(I%)=-DY%(I%)*2
410     PRINT TAB(X%(I%),Y%(I%)) M1$;
420   NEXT I%
430   PROCbat
440   FOR I%=0 TO K
450     PRINT TAB(X%(I%),Y%(I%)) " ";
460   NEXT I%
470   FOR I%=0 TO K
480     X%(I%)=X%(I%)+DX%(I%):Y%(I%)=Y%(I%)+DY%(I%)
490     PRINT TAB(X%(I%),Y%(I%)) M2$;
500   NEXT I%
510   PROCbat
520   FOR I%=0 TO K
```

```
530      PRINT TAB(X%(I%),Y%(I%)) " ";
540      DX%(I%)=RND MOD 3
550      DY%(I%)=RND MOD 3
560    NEXT I%
570    *FX 15,1
580 UNTIL K=-1
590 *FX4,0
600 END
610
620
630 DEF PROCgulp
640    FOR I%=0 TO K
650      IF ABS(BX-X%(I%))>D OR ABS(BY-Y%(I%))>D
         THEN SOUND 1,-15,53,1 ELSE PROCsplat
660    NEXT I%
670 ENDPROC
680
690 DEF PROCbat
700    PRINT TAB(BX,BY) UNBAT$;
710    B=ASC(INKEY$(2))
720    IF B=136 THEN BX=BX-1 ELSE IF B=137 THEN BX=BX+1
       ELSE IF B=138 THEN BY=BY+1 ELSE IF B=139 THEN BY=BY-1
       ELSE IF B=135 THEN PROCgulp
730    IF BY<1 BY=BY+1 ELSE IF BY>29 BY=BY-1
740    IF BX<1 BX=BX+1 ELSE IF BX>38 BX=BX-1
750    PRINT TAB(BX,BY) BAT$;
760 ENDPROC
770
780 DEF PROCsplat
790    ENVELOPE 1,2,1,0,3,1,1,1,127,0,-4,-4,126,4
800    SOUND 0,1,0,2
810    PRINT TAB(X%(I%),Y%(I%))" ";
820    FOR T%=I% TO K-1
830      X%(T%)=X%(T%+1)
840      Y%(T%)=Y%(T%+1)
850    NEXT T%
860    K=K-1
870 ENDPROC
880
890
900 DATA 129,129,195,231,255,231,195,129
910 DATA 36,102,102,102,126,102,102,36
920 DATA 130,130,129,195,199,195,225,227
930 DATA 65,65,129,195,227,195,135,199
940 DATA 231,255,255,239,231,197,137,156
950 DATA 231,255,255,247,231,163,145,57
```

P18 Monster Island

In this program you have landed on a volcanic island and are being pursued by voracious monsters.

Your only hope is to lead the monsters into volcanic pits, over which you can jump. The monsters always move in your direction, so with thought you should survive.

Your position on the island is shown by a small man shaped character. Use keys Z and X to move the man horizontally, / and : to move vertically.

The monsters do not notice you until you move.

Change lines 550 through 600 to improve the response of the game if you win.

COMMANDS

Key in program and type RUN.
Use Z X / : to move man.

```
100 REM Program P18 - Monster Island
110 MODE7
120 PRINT TAB(12,12)"M O N S T E R S"
130 INPUT TAB(5,20) "SPEED(1-5)"SPEED
140 MODE5
150 SPEED=6-SPEED:count=0
160 DEAD=FALSE
170 M=RND(5):P=RND(5)+5
180 DIM MONS(M,2),MAN(2)
190 L$=" "
200 VDU 23,224,31,124,200,248,248,120,60,31:REM Monster
210 VDU 23,225,60,126,255,254,254,62,30,28: REM Pool
220 VDU 23,226,28,28,8,127,28,20,20,54: REM Man
230 VDU 23;8202;0;0;0;:REM Switch cursor off
240 FOR I=1 TO M
250    X=RND(19):Y=RND(31)
260    MONS(I,1)=X:MONS(I,2)=Y
270    COLOUR 1
280    PRINT TAB(X,Y) CHR$(224);
290 NEXT I
300 FOR I=1 TO P
310    X=RND(19):Y=RND(31)
320    COLOUR 3
330    PRINT TAB(X,Y) CHR$(225);
340 NEXT I
```

```
350
360 MAN(1)=RND(19):MAN(2)=RND(31)
370 DX=0:DY=0
380 COLOUR 2
390 PRINT TAB(MAN(1),MAN(2)) CHR$(226);
400 Z=GET
410
420 REPEAT
430    COLOUR 2
440    PRINT TAB(MAN(1),MAN(2)) CHR$(226);
450    DX=INKEY(-98)-INKEY(-67)
460    IF DX PROCmove(1,DX)
470    DX=0
480    DY=INKEY(-73)-INKEY(-105)
490    IF DY PROCmove(2,DY)
500    DY=0
510    count=(count+1) MOD SPEED
520    IF count=0 THEN PROCmonsters
530 UNTIL M=0 OR DEAD
540
550 IF M=0 THEN VDU 19,0,13;0;:SOUND 1,-15,53,100
560 FOR Z=1 TO 300:NEXT Z
570 MODE7
580 *FX15,0
590 END
600
610
620 DEF PROCmove(I,d)
630    IF L$=" " THEN COLOUR 0 ELSE COLOUR 3
640    PRINT TAB(MAN(1),MAN(2)) L$;
650    IF MAN(1)+DX=19 OR MAN(1)+DX=0 DX=0
660    IF MAN(2)+DY=31 OR MAN(2)+DY=0 DY=0
670    L=FNchar(MAN(1)+DX,MAN(2)+DY)
680    IF L=224 PROCdie:ENDPROC
690    IF L=225 THEN L$=CHR$(225) ELSE L$=" "
700    COLOUR 2
710    PRINT TAB(MAN(1)+DX,MAN(2)+DY) CHR$(226);
720    MAN(1)=MAN(1)+DX
730    MAN(2)=MAN(2)+DY
740 ENDPROC
750
760 DEF PROCdie
770    VDU19,0,9;0;
780    SOUND 1,-15,23,100
790    DEAD=TRUE
800    FOR Z=1 TO 300:NEXT Z
810 ENDPROC
820
```

```
 830 DEF PROCmonsters
 840    FOR I=1 TO M
 850       CX=SGN(MAN(1)-MONS(I,1))
 860       CY=SGN(MAN(2)-MONS(I,2))
 870       L=FNchar(MONS(I,1)+CX,MONS(I,2)+CY)
 880       IF L=225 PROCmonskill:GOTO 970
 890       COLOUR 1
 900       IF L=226 PRINT TAB(MONS(I,1)+CX,MONS(I,2)+CY)
          CHR$(224);:COLOUR 0:PRINT TAB(MONS(I,1),MONS(I,2)) " ";:
          PROCdie:ENDPROC
 910       COLOUR 0
 920       PRINT TAB(MONS(I,1),MONS(I,2)) " ";
 930       COLOUR 1
 940       PRINT TAB(MONS(I,1)+CX,MONS(I,2)+CY) CHR$(224);
 950       MONS(I,1)=MONS(I,1)+CX
 960       MONS(I,2)=MONS(I,2)+CY
 970    NEXT I
 980 ENDPROC
 990
1000 DEF PROCmonskill
1010    SOUND 0,-15,10,2
1020    COLOUR 0
1030    PRINT TAB(MONS(I,1),MONS(I,2))" ";
1040    IF I=M THEN M=M-1:ENDPROC
1050    FOR J=I TO M-1
1060       MONS(J,1)=MONS(J+1,1)
1070       MONS(J,2)=MONS(J+1,2)
1080    NEXT J
1090    M=M-1
1100 ENDPROC
1110
1120 DEF FNchar(u,v)
1130    PRINT TAB(u,v);
1140    A%=135
1150 =(USR(&FFF4) AND &FF00)/&100
```

P19 Battleships

This is an implementation of the old schoolboy game of battleships. The game is played in Mode 5 using a mixture of graphics and user defined characters.

The game opens by displaying a map of an area of sea in which an enemy fleet is deployed. The fleet consists of four battleships, eight cruisers and sixteen destroyers.

The map is displayed as a 26 by 18 square grid. A battleship occupies three contiguous grid locations, a cruiser two locations and a destroyer one location.

Thus out of a possible 486 squares, 44 (or approximately 10%) are occupied by enemy ships.

The positions of the enemy fleet are displayed on the screen when the computer allocates each ships position, but, when the whole fleet has been placed, the computer hides the fleet. You therefore have a few seconds in which to memorise the fleet positions.

Once the board is set up, the computer prompts you to enter a grid reference. If the position is occupied by a ship:

    a red flash is printed on the screen
    a hit noise is generated
    a hit score is allocated

If the position is not occupied by a ship:

    a white flash is painted on the screen
    a miss noise is generated
    a miss score is allocated

At the end of the game a score is given. I have yet to get a positive score.

To improve the game, make the ships larger; this would give the player a better chance of achieving a good score.

COMMANDS

Key in program and type RUN.
Watch the screen carefully, then follow instructions.

```
100 REM Program P19 - Battleships
110 MODE 5
120 DIM POSNS(44,2)
130 VDU 23,225,0,0,12,12,0,0,0,0
140 VDU 23,224,73,42,28,63,248,28,18,17
150 ENVELOPE 1,50,100,0,-100,10,100,10,100,-100,0,-10,126,0
160 VDU 19,0,4;0;
170 VDU 5
180 FOR X=64 TO 1216 STEP 64
190   MOVE X,128:DRAW X,960
200 NEXT X
210 FOR Y=128 TO 960 STEP 32
220   MOVE 64,Y:DRAW 1216,Y
230 NEXT Y
240 MOVE 64,1000
250 FOR I=1 TO 18
260   PRINT CHR$(64+I);
270 NEXT I
280 MOVE 0,960
290 FOR I=1 TO 26
300   PRINT CHR$(64+I);CHR$(8);CHR$(10);
310 NEXT I
320 REM Set up board
330 L=0
340 GCOL 0,2
350 S$=CHR$(225)
360 FOR battle=1 TO 4
370   X=RND(14)+2:Y=RND(22)+3
380   DX=RND(3)-2:DY=RND(3)-2
390   IF DX=0 AND DY=0 THEN DX=1
400   FOR I=0 TO 2
410     PROCcheck(X+DX*I,Y+DY*I)
420   NEXT I
430   IF position_free PRINT TAB(X,Y)S$;TAB(X+DX,Y+DY)S$;
      TAB(X+DX*2,Y+DY*2)S$:PROCposns(3) ELSE battle=battle-1
440 NEXT battle
450
460 FOR cruiser=1 TO 8
470   X=RND(14)+2:Y=RND(22)+3
480   DX=RND(3)-2:DY=RND(3)-2
490   IF DX=0 AND DY=0 THEN DX=1
500   FOR I=0 TO1
510     PROCcheck(X+DX*I,Y+DY*I)
520   NEXT I
530   IF position_free PRINT TAB(X,Y)S$;TAB(X+DX,Y+DY)S$:
      PROCposns(2) ELSE cruiser=cruiser-1
540 NEXT cruiser
550
```

```
560 FOR destroyer=1 TO 16
570   X=RND(14)+2:Y=RND(22)+3
580   PROCcheck(X,Y)
590   IF position_free PRINT TAB(X,Y)S$;:POSNS(L+1,1)=X:
      POSNS(L+1,2)=Y:L=L+1 ELSE destroyer=destroyer-1
600 NEXT destroyer
610   VDU 19,2,4;0;
620 hits=0:miss=0
630 REPEAT
640   PROCgetposn
650   PROCcheck(X,Y)
660   IF position_free PROCmiss(X,Y):miss=miss+1
      ELSE hits=hits+1:PROChit(X,Y)
670 UNTIL hits=44
680 MODE 7
690 PRINT TAB(0,12) "SCORE="hits-miss
700 END
710
720 DEF PROChit(X,Y)
730   GCOL0,1
740   PRINT TAB(X,Y) CHR$(224)
750   SOUND &10,1,100,100
760 ENDPROC
770
780 DEF PROCmiss(X,Y)
790   GCOL0,3
800   PRINT TAB(X,Y) CHR$(224)
810   SOUND &11,-15,53,10
820 ENDPROC
830
840 DEF PROCcheck(X,Y)
850   position_free=TRUE
860   FOR I=1 TO 44
870     IF X=POSNS(I,1) AND Y=POSNS(I,2)
        THEN position_free=FALSE:I=44
880     NEXT I
890 ENDPROC
900
910 DEF PROCposns(K)
920   FOR I=1 TO K
930     POSNS(L+I,1)=X+DX*(I-1):POSNS(L+I,2)=Y+DY*(I-1)
940     NEXT I
950   L=L+K
960 ENDPROC
970
980 DEF PROCgetposn
990   VDU 4:VDU 28,0,31,19,28
```

```
1000    MOVE 0,32
1010     PRINT "HITS= ";STR$(hits)
1020    INPUT TAB(0,30)"ROW= "R$,"COLUMN= "C$
1030    X=ASC(C$)-64:Y=ASC(R$)-63
1040    VDU 26
1050    VDU 5
1060 ENDPROC
```

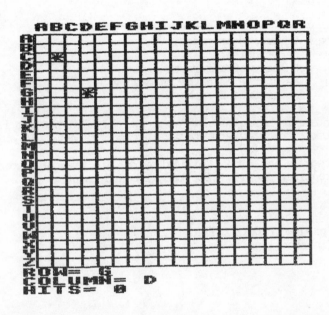

P20 Loan Repayment Period

This program uses the formula

$$T = \frac{-1}{N} \left[\frac{\log\left(1 - \frac{P.R}{N.A}\right)}{\log\left(1 + \frac{R}{N}\right)} \right]$$

Where T= period in years.
P= principal.
R= rate of interest.
N= number of payments each year.
A= amount of each payment.

This could be calculated by using a calculator, but it is far quicker to allow the computer to do the work for you.

This program could be improved by designing a more robust input routine, to check for bad keyboard input.

COMMANDS

Key in program and type RUN.
Follow instructions.

```
100 REM Program P20 - Loan Repayment Period
110 MODE7
120 PRINT "If you are about to take out a loan "
130 PRINT "it could be useful to consider how long"
140 PRINT "it will be before the loan is repaid."
150 PRINT "To use this program you must input "
160 PRINT TAB(5)"Amount borrowed"
170 PRINT TAB(5)"Annual interest rate"
180 PRINT TAB(5)"Number of payments per year"
190 PRINT TAB(5)"Amount of payments"
200 PRINT ''"Press any key to continue"
210 Z=GET
220 CLS
230 INPUT TAB(5)"Amount borrowed £"P
240 INPUT TAB(5)"Annual interest rate (%) "rate:
    rate=rate/100
250 INPUT TAB(5)"Number of payments per year "N
260 INPUT TAB(5)"Amount of payments £" A
270 time=-LOG(1-P*rate/N/A)/LOG(1+rate/N)/N
280 year=INT(time)
290 months=INT(12*(time-year)+.5)
300 PRINT "Loan will be paid off in ";year;" years and "';
        months;" months"
310 END
```

P21 Wordprocessor

We can consider this program to be a skeleton wordprocessor. In its present configuration, the wordprocessor can handle three pages of sixty-six lines of forty characters each.

The wordprocessor is in a pretty basic state, but the capability for expansion is there.

The program is made up of a series of routines; the first lines, 110 to 170, allocate enough memory for three pages of text.

The input routine occupies lines 190 to 340. As each letter key is pressed it is passed to the control procedure PROCcontrol. This procedure checks whether a character pressed is a "control code" or not. At the moment only two control codes are recognised:

Control P.   This code causes the print procedure to be called, which prints out text entered so far. The print procedure includes two lines 660 and 670, to set up the printer. Lines 680 to 770 send the text to the printer.

Delete.   If the delete key has been pressed, the character is deleted both from the screen and from the text in memory.

One other procedure has been implemented, PROCwordwrap on lines 400 to 510. This procedure is called at the end of a line if the last character is not a space. The procedure cuts off the last word on the line and places it at the beginning of the next line.

Other routines which could be entered are:

Right justification.
Cursor control.
Insert/overwrite characters.

COMMANDS

Key in program and type RUN.
Wait until the screen clears then enter text.

To delete last character, press delete, note that this
routine cannot delete past the beginning of the line.

To print your text make sure that printer is powered on and
press control and the letter P together.

```
100 REM Program P21 - Wordprocessor
110 DIM page$(66,3)
120 FOR I=1 TO 3
130  FOR J=1 TO 66
140   page$(J,I)=STRING$(40,"*")
150   page$(J,I)=""
160  NEXT J
170 NEXT I
180
190 MODE 7
200 line$=""
210 FOR page=1 TO 3
220   FOR line_number=1 TO 66
230     page$(line_number,page)=line$
240     len=LEN(page$(line_number,page))
250     PRINT page$(line_number,page);
260     FOR character_no=len TO 39
270       letter$=GET$
280       PROCcontrol(letter$)
290       IF NOT ctrl_chr THEN PRINT letter$;:
              page$(line_number,page)=page$(line_number,page)+
                                  letter$
300     NEXT character_no
310     IF letter$<>" " THEN PROCword_wrap ELSE line$=""
320   NEXT line_number
330   PRINT STRING$(40,"_")
340 NEXT page
350 SOUND 1,-15,53,20
360 PRINT "No room left - Print your text"
370 PROCprint
380 END
390
400 DEF PROCword_wrap
410  line$=page$(line_number,page)
420  REPEAT
430    X=INSTR(line$," ")
440    IF X>0 line$=MID$(line$,X+1)
450  UNTIL X=0
460  len=LEN(line$)
470  page$(line_number,page)=
            LEFT$(page$(line_number,page),40-len)
```

```
480   V=VPOS
490   PRINT TAB(0,V-1) STRING$(40," ");
500   PRINT TAB(0,V-1)page$(line_number,page)
510 ENDPROC
520
530 DEF PROCcontrol(c$)
540   ctrl_chr=TRUE
550   REM NON CONTROL CHRS
560    IF ASC(c$)>31 AND ASC(c$)<126 THEN ctrl_chr=FALSE:
      ENDPROC
570   REM BACKSPACE/DELETE
580    IF ASC(c$)=127 THEN PROCdelete:ENDPROC
590   REM PRINT : CTRL-P
600    IF ASC(c$)=16 THEN PROCprint:ENDPROC
610   REM Other control codes here
620 ENDPROC
630
640
650 DEF PROCprint
660   *FX5,1
670   *FX8,4
680   VDU 2
690   FOR I=1 TO page
700     FOR J=1 TO line_number
710       FOR K=1 TO LEN(page$(J,I))
720         VDU1,ASC(MID$(page$(J,I),K,1))
730       NEXT K
740       VDU1,13
750     NEXT J
760   NEXT I
770   VDU 3
771   character_no=character_no-1
780 ENDPROC
790
800 DEF PROCdelete
810   PRINT CHR$(127);
820   l=LEN(page$(line_number,page))-1
830   page$(line_number,page)=
              LEFT$(page$(line_number,page),l)
840   character_no=character_no-2
850 ENDPROC
```

This program shows some of the features
of a word processor. It could be used
for the production of short letters and
documents.Mistakes can be corrected and
word wrap is included. When necessary
the text can be printed out to the
printer. The program is at present set
up for a parallel printer with a
transmit rate of 1200 baud. The program
does not save the text onto tape but
this could easily be done. Other
features which could be added would be
paragraphing, centering, more editing
features and right hand justification.
The maximum length of text is 3 pages
of 66 lines of 40 characters. When a
page of text is typed in, a row of "_"'s
is printed onto the screen to let the
user know where he/she is. If you are
using paper of a different length, then
simply amend lines 130 and 220. To
delete a character press the delete
key, to print the text press ctrl-P.

P22 Depreciation

This program can be used to calculate the depreciation in the value of an asset arising from normal use through time.

The program shows the effect of two common methods of calculating this depreciation.

1. The Straight Line Method

Under this method, a fixed amount (a percentage of the initial value) is written off annually. The resulting graph is then a straight line of value against year. For example, if initial value was $8000, say, and 25% of the original cost is written off each year, then we have:

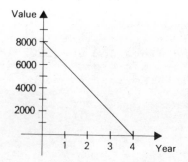

2. Diminishing Balance Method

Under this method, a percentage of the value of the asset at the beginning of the year is written off at the end of the year. This gives a curve like:

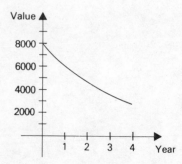

The program presents the two depreciation methods in the
form of a table, showing amount to be written off over a
period of years.

COMMANDS

Key in program and type RUN.
Follow instructions.

```
100 REM Program P22 - Depreciation
110 MODE7
120 PRINT TAB(2,2);"Depreciation calculations"
130 PRINT '''
140 PRINT "There are 2 common methods of"
150 PRINT "calculating the amount of depreciation"
160 PRINT "for a given period. These are:"
170 PRINT ''"1. The straight line method"
180 PRINT "2. The diminishing balance method"
190 PRINT ''"This program shows depreciation over"
200 PRINT "a fixed period, using both methods."
210 PRINT ''"Press any key to continue"
220 g=GET
230 CLS
240 INPUT "Value of asset on acquisition",init_value
250 INPUT "Fixed amount to be written off annually ",amount
260 INPUT "Percentage to be written off annually   ",
            percentage
270 INPUT "No of years to be presented ",years
280 PRINT ''"Press any key to continue"
290 g=GET
300 CLS
310 @%=LEN(STR$(init_value))
320 val_2=init_value
330 PRINT "Year";TAB(15);"Value 1";TAB(30);"Value 2"
340 FOR I=1 TO years
350    val_1=init_value - amount*I
360    IF val_1<0 THEN val_1=0
370    val_2=val_2*(100 - percentage)/100
380    IF val_2<0 THEN val_2=0
390    PRINT I;TAB(15);INT(val_1);TAB(30);INT(val_2)
400 NEXT I
410 END
```

P23 Four-weekly Moving Average

When attempting to measure trends in sales data it can be useful to plot the sales data along with a continually updated average of the last four weeks' sales.

This program performs such a task, with the sales data held in the form of data statements. Note that the data is terminated by a negative sale.

COMMANDS

Key in program and type RUN.
Follow instructions.

```
100 REM Program P23 - Four-weekly Moving Average
110 DIM sales(53),movav(50)
120 MODE7
130  PRINT "This program can be used to help you"
140 PRINT "to forecast sales based on a graph of "
150 PRINT "a 4-weekly moving average."
160 PRINT '"This can be a fairly useful program,"
170 PRINT "but bear in mind that it does not"
180 PRINT "consider seasonal variations."
190 PRINT'''
200 PRINT "Data is held in DATA statements, and"
210 PRINT "up to 52 weeks can be handled."
220 PRINT '"If necessary escape from the program"
230 PRINT "and add to the data."
240 PRINT '"Hit any other key to continue"
250 x=GET
260
270 REM Scale the data
280 no=0:max_sales=0
290 REPEAT
300     no=no+1
310     READ sales(no)
320     IF max_sales<sales(no) THEN max_sales=sales(no)
330 UNTIL sales(no)<0
340
350 FOR I=4 TO no-1
360    movav(I-3)=(sales(I)+sales(I-1)+sales(I-2)+sales(I-3))/4
370 NEXT I
380
390
```

```
400 REM Draw axes
410 MODE 5
420 VDU 19,0,7;0;19,3,0;0;
430 COLOUR1
440 PRINT '" Weekly Sales - 1982"
450 MOVE 16,0:DRAW 16,1023
460 MOVE 0,100:DRAW 1279,100
470 X=0
480 FOR I=1 TO 13
490     FOR J=1 TO 3
500        MOVE 16+X+J*24,90
510        DRAW 16+X+J*24,110
520     NEXT J
530     MOVE 16+X+96,80
540     DRAW 16+X+96,120
550     X=X+96
560 NEXT I
570 PRINT TAB(1,30)"  2   4   6   8  10  12";
580
590 vert_unit=max_sales DIV 20
600 VDU5
610 FOR I=1 TO 20
630     MOVE 12,100+I*40
640     DRAW 30,100+I*40
650     IF I MOD 4=0  THENPRINT;I*vert_unit;
660 NEXT I
670
680 scale=40/vert_unit
690 MOVE 40,scale*sales(1)+100
700 GCOL 0,2
710 FOR I= 2 TO no-1
720     DRAW I*24,scale*sales(I)+100
730 NEXT I
740
750 GCOL 0,1
760 MOVE 64,scale*movav(1)+100
770 FOR I=2 TO no-4
780     DRAW I*24+64,scale*movav(I)+100
790 NEXT I
800
810 X=GET:REM wait till key is pressed
820 DATA 112,224,115,212,118,215,113,214,115,216,112,
        223,126,224,125,265,145,293,116,216,193,293
830 DATA 187,315,220,354,232,367,198,354,267,365,287,
        398,254,254,176,234,144,201,101,350,190,483
840 DATA 190,190
850 DATA -9
```

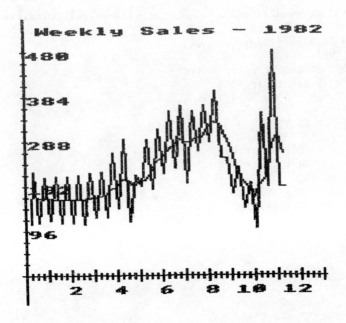

P24 Mailing List Creation

This program is used to set up a mailing list on tape.

It cannot be used to add or insert or delete a name to the mailing list. It is left as an exercise to the reader to write such a program. (But see the Christmas card and maintenance program.)

COMMANDS

Key in program and type RUN.
Follow instructions.

Ensure that tape is correctly placed in recorder and that the power is on, etc.

Enter "END" to finish program.

Note :   you will have to enter something (press RETURN) for the INPUTs on lines 170 and 180 to finish program correctly.

```
100 REM Program P24 - Mailing List Creation
110 ch_no=OPENOUT("mail_list")
120 REPEAT
130    CLS
140    PRINT "Enter name and address,use"
150    PRINT "name=end to finish"
160    INPUT '"Name - "name$
170    INPUT '"Address_1 - "address_1$,"Address_2 - "
              address_2$,"Address_3 - "address_3$
180    INPUT '"Post Code - "p_code$
190    PRINT#ch_no,name$,address_1$,address_2$,address_3$,
       p_code$
200 UNTIL name$="end"
210 CLOSE#ch_no
220 END
```

P25 Mailing List Print

This program requires the use of a printer, to print the
mailing list. It is possible to obtain sticky labels which
could be used for the addresses. This saves the problem of
cutting the paper up and using glue.

If you are using sticky labels, then lines 260 and 280 can
be used to ensure that each address starts at the correct
position on the label.

COMMANDS

Key in program.
Ensure that the tape is ready.
Type RUN and follow instructions.

```
100 REM Program P25 - Mailing List Print
110 MODE 7
120 PRINT "This program prints the mailing list"
130 PRINT "onto sticky labels"
140 PRINT '"Load and rewind correct tape"
150 PRINT "Make sure that labels are in printer "
160 PRINT "and are aligned "
170 PRINT '"Press any key when ready"
180 Z=GET
190 CLS
200 PRINT "Press PLAY on tape"
210 ch_no=OPENIN("mail_list")
220 VDU 2:REM printer on
230 REPEAT
240   REM Lines 260 and 280 are used to position printer
250   INPUT#ch_no,name$,address_1$,address_2$,address_3$,
      p_code$
260   IF name$="end" THEN 300
270   FOR I=1 TO 3:PRINT " ":NEXT I
280   PRINT name$,',address_1$,',,address_2$,'
            ,address_3$,',p_code$
290   FOR I=1 TO 3:PRINT " ":NEXT I
300 UNTIL name$="end"
310 VDU 3:REM Printer off
320 CLOSE#ch_no
330 END
```

P26, P27 and P28 Stock Control

These three programs form a rudimentary stock control system. Program 26 is used to set up the stock control file initially. Notice that in its present form there are only ten stock items. But I am sure that the reader would be able to amend the program to allow the inclusion of more than ten items.

Program P26 is similar to program P24, Mailing List Creation. The user must ensure that the tape is in the recorder.

Program P27 is used to record all transactions, both additions to and withdrawals from stocks. The program in its present state, does not verify the data being entered, this would be a useful feature.

Program P28, the stock update and report program, is a rather complicated program and should be entered fairly carefully. I have attempted to make this program fairly self documented through the use of REM and PRINT statements.

It is not possible to use two tape files simultaneously on the BBC microcomputer, therefore the first thing that P28 does is to read the stock file into memory for updating. The transaction file is then loaded into the recorder and is used to update the stockfile in memory.

The last section of the program requires the use of a printer to obtain a printout of all items to be recorded. If you do not require a printout, then remove lines 490 and 560.

The full stock control system is shown on the following diagram.

COMMANDS
Have some blank tapes ready.
Key in programs and type RUN.
Follow instructions.

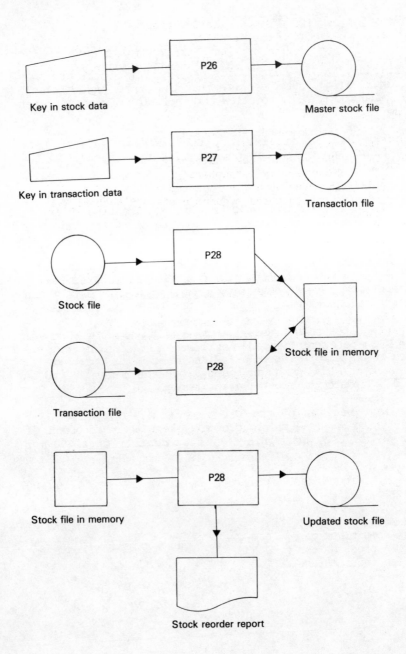

Key in stock data

P26

Master stock file

Key in transaction data

P27

Transaction file

Stock file

P28

Transaction file

P28

Stock file in memory

Stock file in memory

P28

Updated stock file

Stock reorder report

```
100 REM Program P26 - Stock File Creation
110 stocks=OPENOUT("stock_file")
120 PRINT "This program sets up a stock file of 10"
130 PRINT "stock items. It can be amended similarly"
140 PRINT "to the mailing list program to be more"
150 PRINT "flexible"
160 FOR I=1 TO 10
170   CLS
180   INPUT "Stock number "numbers_1
190   INPUT "Description "desc$
200   INPUT "Number in stock "numbers_2
210   INPUT "Reorder level "numbers_3
220   INPUT "Reorder quantity "numbers_4
230   PRINT#stocks,numbers_1,desc$,numbers_2,numbers_3,
      numbers_4
240 NEXT I
250 CLOSE#stocks
260 END


100 REM Program P27 - Transaction File Creation
110 trans=OPENOUT("transfile")
120 PRINT "This program sets up a transaction file"
130 PRINT "for use in the stock control system"
160 REPEAT
161   CLS
170   PRINT "Enter transaction details "
180   PRINT "Enter -9 for last stock number"
190   PRINT '''
200   INPUT "Stock_no" s
210   INPUT "Code 1-withdrawal, 2-addition "c
220   INPUT "Quantity "q
230   IF s=-9 THEN CLOSE#trans ELSE PRINT#trans,s,c,q
240 UNTIL s=-9
250 END
```

```
100 REM Program P28 - Stock File Update and Report
110 REM This program is written as a series of modules,
          solving each part of the problem
120 REM The first section sets up space for the stock file
130 REM The stock file is held in memory in the form of 2 arrays,
          the first being a string array to hold the descriptions
140 REM The other is a 2 dimensional array containing the
          numeric data of the stock file
150 DIM description$(10),numbers(10,4)
160 REM We now read in the stock file
170 MODE 7
180 PRINT "Load stock file tape into cassette and  rewind"
190 PRINT "Press any key when ready"
200 a$=GET$
210 PRINT "Press PLAY on recorder"
220 stocks=OPENIN("stock_file")
230 FOR I=1 TO 10
240     INPUT#stocks,numbers(I,1),description$(I),numbers(I,2),
          numbers(I,3),numbers(I,4)
250 NEXT I
260 CLOSE#stocks
270 CLS
280 PRINT "The stock file is now in memory"
290 PRINT"Remove stock file and load transaction file,":
          "rewind if necessary"
300 PRINT"Hit any key when ready"
310 a$=GET$
320 PRINT"Updating stock file"
330 trans=OPENIN("transfile")
340 REM The following section of code updates the
          stock file in memory
350 REPEAT
360     INPUT#trans,I,code,quantity
370     IF code=1 THEN numbers(I,2)=numbers(I,2)-quantity
          ELSE numbers(I,2)=numbers(I,2)+quantity
380 UNTIL EOF#trans
390 REM Stock file updated
400 CLOSE#trans
410 REM The following section of code prints all items to be
          reordered, and also writes the new version of the
          stock file to tape
420 CLS
430 PRINT"Load fresh tape into recorder and rewind"
440 PRINT"Ensure that printer is set up properly"
450 PRINT"Hit any key when ready"
460 a$=GET$
470 CLS
```

```
480 PRINT"Processing......"
490 VDU 2:REM start printer
500 PRINT"Items to be reordered:"
510 new_stock=OPENOUT("stock_file")
520 FOR I=1 TO 10
530     PRINT#new_stock,numbers(I,1),description$(I),
        numbers(I,2),numbers(I,3),numbers(I,4)
540     IF numbers(I,2)<numbers(I,3) THEN
        PRINT numbers(I,1),description$(I),
        numbers(I,2),numbers(I,3),numbers(I,4)
550 NEXT I
560 VDU 3:REM stop printout
570 CLOSE#new_stock
580 CLS
590 PRINT
    "Job finished - remove tape and label with today's date"
600 END
```

P29 VAT Calculator

This program allows you to use the BBC micro as an aid in calculating VAT.

The results of the calculation are presented, rounded to the nearest penny.

The user has the option of changing the current rate of VAT from 15%.

Note that none of the data are saved.

COMMANDS

Key in program and type RUN.
Enter data as required.

```
100 REM Program P29 - VAT Calculator
110 MODE 7
120 PRINT TAB(15,12)"V A T"
130 PRINT TAB(8,14)"C A L C U L A T O R"
140 Z=INKEY(300)
150 CLS
160 vat=.15
170 PRINT "Current rate of VAT is 15%"
180 PRINT "Do you wish to change this";
190 INPUT res$
200 IF LEFT$(res$,1)="Y" THEN
    INPUT "New rate (%) " rate:vat=rate/100
210
220 REPEAT
230    CLS
240    INPUT ´´´"Cost of item £"cost
250    PRINT ´´"VAT =          £";FNround(cost*vat)
260    PRINT ´´"Total cost    £";FNround(cost*(1+vat))
270    INPUT ´´´"Another run ",res$
280 UNTIL LEFT$(res$,1)<>"Y"
290 END
300
310 DEF FNround(X)=INT(X*100+.5)/100
```

Cost of item £35

VAT =   £5.25

Total cost   £40.25

Another run

P30 True Rate of Interest

This program uses a simple approach to calculating the true rate of interest on a loan. The program assumes that repayments are made on a monthly basis.

To calculate the true rate of interest, we compute the amount of pound-months that have been borrowed. (One pound-month is equivalent to borrowing one pound for one month, or fifty pence for two months.) This is done in lines 280 to 310. We now know the equivalent amount borrowed as a percentage. We then multiply this ratio by twelve.

COMMANDS

Key in program and type RUN.
Follow instructions.

```
100 REM Program P30 - True Rate of Interest
110 @%=&2020A
120 MODE 7
130 PRINT "This program computes the TRUE RATE OF"
140 PRINT "INTEREST for a loan transaction."
150 PRINT '"The program requires the amount"
160 PRINT "borrowed, the annual interest rate"
170 PRINT "and the number of months over which"
180 PRINT "the loan is taken. The program assumes"
190 PRINT "simple interest only."
200 PRINT ''
210 INPUT "Amount borrowed "amount
220 INPUT "Annual interest rate (%) "rate
230 rate=rate/100
240 INPUT "Number of months "number
250 interest=amount*rate*number/12
260 capital_payback=amount/number
270 REM calculate interest on monthly basis
280 borrowed=0
290 FOR I=1 TO number
300   borrowed=borrowed+(amount - capital_payback*(I-1))
310 NEXT I
320 true_interest_rate = 12*100*interest/borrowed
330 PRINT "True interest rate is "true_interest_rate"%"
340 END
```

P31 Simple Tax Calculator

This is a useful program for keeping an eye on the taxman. It is based on the WHICH? magazine tax calculator for 1981-82, and saves any complicated arithmetic. It cannot be used if you are involved with higher rates of tax, but it could be amended.

The tax rate is used on line 720.

To use the program you require your P60 form and your notice of coding.

Note however that neither the author nor the publisher will accept any responsibility in your negotiations with the taxman.

Notice the use of MODE 7 colours in this program.

COMMANDS

Key in program and type RUN.
Follow instructions.

```
100 REM Program P31 - Simple Tax Calculator
110 MODE 7
120 PRINT ''"This program is based on the simple"
130 PRINT "tax calculator used by WHICH?"
140 PRINT "The data used is UK tax data for year"
150 PRINT "1981-1982"
155 PRINT ''''"PRESS ANY KEY TO CONTINUE"
160 Z=GET
170 CLS
180 PRINT "Page 1"
190 PRINT "Enter INCOME for period 6 April 1981"
200 PRINT "to 5 April 1982"
210 PRINT '"Earnings - enter before-tax earnings of"
220 PRINT "husband and wife after deducting "
230 PRINT "contributions to employers' pension"
240 PRINT "scheme (P60 form). Include as earnings"
250 PRINT "any expenses you or your wife have to"
260 PRINT "pay tax on, and the value used for "
270 PRINT "working out tax on any fringe benefits"
280 PRINT "you or your wife get ";CHR$(129);
290 INPUT "£"i_1
300 PRINT '"Pensions :enter taxable amounts"
310 PRINT "received ";CHR$(129);
320 INPUT "£"i_2
```

```
330 PRINT '"Investment Income:"
340 PRINT "Enter interest not taxed before you get"
350 PRINT "it. For example, interest from bank"
360 PRINT "deposit accounts. The interest is "
370 PRINT "normally taxed on a preceding year"
380 PRINT "basis - in which case enter income for"
390 PRINT "period 6/4/80 to 5/4/81 ";CHR$(129);
400 INPUT "£" i_3
405 A=i_1+i_2+i_3
410 CLS
420 PRINT "Page 2"
430 PRINT "Enter OUTGOINGS and ALLOWANCES for"
440 PRINT "6/4/81 to 5/4/82"
450 PRINT '"Expenses in your employment, paid out"
460 PRINT "of your earnings ";CHR$(129);
470 INPUT "£" allow_1
480 PRINT '"Expenses in your wife's employment"
490 PRINT "paid out of your wife's earnings";
          CHR$(129);
500 INPUT "£" allow_2
510 PRINT '"Interest which qualifies for tax relief"'
          CHR$(129);
520 INPUT "£" allow_3
530 PRINT '"Personal allowance (£1375 single, "
540 PRINT "£2145 married) or age allowance"
550 PRINT "(£1820 single, £2895 married)";CHR$(129);
560 INPUT"£" allow_4
570 PRINT '"Wife's earned income allowance (£1375)"
580 PRINT "or her before-tax earnings less any"
590 PRINT "allowable expenses in her job, "
600 PRINT "whichever is less) ";CHR$(129);
610 INPUT"£" allow_5
620 PRINT'"Other allowances ";CHR$(129);
625 INPUT "£" allow_6
630 B=allow_1+allow_2+allow_3+allow_4+allow_5+allow_6
700 CLS
710 taxable_income=A-B
720 tax_liable=taxable_income*.3
721 PRINT "Page 3"''
730 PRINT "Enter tax already paid:"
740 PRINT '"Add up tax paid by husband and wife"
750 PRINT "under PAYE (get from P60), and any "
760 PRINT "other tax for 1981-82 already paid on"
770 PRINT "the investment income you've already"
780 PRINT "entered above";CHR$(129);
790 INPUT "£" tax_already_paid
791 PRINT''''
```

```
800 IF tax_liable>=tax_already_paid THEN
    PRINT "Tax you owe =f";CHR$(129);
    tax_liable-tax_already_paid
810 IF tax_liable<tax_already_paid THEN
    PRINT "Tax rebate due =£";CHR$(129);
    tax_already_paid-tax_liable
820 PRINT "(adjust for any tax under- or over-paid)"
830 PRINT "in previous years"
840 END
```

P32 Loan Repayments

I use this program to try to dissuade myself from buying
something using a loan from a finance house.

It can be quite illuminating to have a note of the full
schedule of repayments for a loan and how slowly the amount
owed drops.

If the interest rate changes during the period of a loan
then simply run the program again as if you had taken out a
new loan, with a reduced amount borrowed.

COMMANDS

Key in program and type RUN.
Follow instructions.

```
100 REM Program P32 - Loan Repayments
110 MODE 4
120 PRINT ''"This program can be used to plan"
130 PRINT "the repayments schedule for a loan."
140 PRINT "The loan is paid back at a fixed "
150 PRINT "monthly rate. The interest is also"
160 PRINT "fixed. The program produces the "
170 PRINT "repayments table."
180 PRINT '"If a printer is fixed then ensure that"
190 PRINT "the correct *FX commands have been"
200 PRINT "executed."
210 INPUT '"Enter amount of loan "amount
220 INPUT '"Enter monthly repayments "repayment
230 INPUT '"Enter monthly interest rate (%) "interest
240 INPUT '"Month number (1-12) "month
250 INPUT "Year "year
260 INPUT "Do you wish a printout (Y/N) "ans$
270 IF ans$="Y" THEN VDU 2
280 CLS
290 PRINT "Year","Month","Amount","Amount"
300 PRINT " "," "," ","paid","owed"
310 IF ans$<>"Y" THEN VDU 28,0,31,39,4:VDU 14
320 paid=0
330 REPEAT
340    month=month+1
350    IF month=13 THEN year=year+1:month=1
360    amount=amount+amount*interest/100
370    amount=amount-repayment
380    paid=paid+repayment
390    @%=4
```

```
400   PRINT year,SPC(4)month;"   ";
410   @%=&20208
420   PRINT paid,amount
430 UNTIL amount<0
440 VDU 3
450 VDU 15
```

This program can be used to plan
the repayments schedule for a loan.
The loan is paid back at a fixed
monthly rate. The interest is also
fixed. The program produces the
repayments table.
If a printer is fixed then ensure that
the correct *FX commands have been
executed
Enter amount of loan 150
Enter monthly repayments 6
Enter monthly interest rate (%) 2.5
Month number (1-12) 11
Year 1981
Do you wish a printout (Y/N) Y

Year	Month	Amount Paid	Amount Owed
1981	12	6.00	147.75
1982	1	12.00	145.44
1982	2	18.00	143.08
1982	3	24.00	140.66
1982	4	30.00	138.17
1982	5	36.00	135.63
1982	6	42.00	133.02
1982	7	48.00	130.34
1982	8	54.00	127.60
1982	9	60.00	124.79
1982	10	66.00	121.91
1982	11	72.00	118.96
1982	12	78.00	115.93
1983	1	84.00	112.83
1983	2	90.00	109.65
1983	3	96.00	106.39
1983	4	102.00	103.05
1983	5	108.00	99.63
1983	6	114.00	96.12
1983	7	120.00	92.52
1983	8	126.00	88.84
1983	9	132.00	85.06
1983	10	138.00	81.19
1983	11	144.00	77.21
1983	12	150.00	73.15
1984	1	156.00	68.97
1984	2	162.00	64.70
1984	3	168.00	60.32
1984	4	174.00	55.82
1984	5	180.00	51.22
1984	6	186.00	46.50
1984	7	192.00	41.66
1984	8	198.00	36.70
1984	9	204.00	31.62
1984	10	210.00	26.41
1984	11	216.00	21.07
1984	12	222.00	15.60
1985	1	228.00	9.99
1985	2	234.00	4.24
1985	3	240.00	-1.66

P33 Monthly Accounts

In our household, one task that has to be done is the monthly budget.

The program prompts the user to enter all his outgoings and income, and ends up with a printout onto paper or screen of a monthly balance sheet.

The program is self explanatory.

COMMAND

Key in program and type RUN.
If you are using a printer ensure that correct *FX commands have been issued.

```
100 REM Program P33 - Monthly Accounts
110 @%=&2020A
120 MODE7
130 PRINT TAB(5,12)"M O N T H L Y   A C C O U N T S"
140 Z=INKEY(300)
150 CLS
160 PRINT "This program helps you to budget"
170 PRINT "your monthly outgoings and incomings."
180 PRINT "The program prompts you to enter your "
190 PRINT "financial dealings and produces a "
200 PRINT "balance sheet for the next month."
210 PRINT "If you have a printer then the balance"
220 PRINT "sheet will also be sent to the printer."
230 PRINT '"Ensure that printer is set up if needed."
240 PRINT ''"Press any key to continue"
250 Z=GET
260 CLS
270 FOR I=1 TO 25:PRINT CHR$(129):NEXT I
280 PRINT TAB(1,1)"Regular outgoings-";
290 INPUT TAB(1,3)"Mortgage repayment " mort
300 INPUT TAB(1,4)"Rates payment " rates
310 INPUT TAB(1,5)"Rent payment " rent
320 INPUT TAB(1,6)"Electricity " electric
330 INPUT TAB(1,7)"Gas " gas
340 credit=0:L=9
350 REPEAT
360    INPUT TAB(1,L)"Credit repayments (0 to finish) " c
370    credit=credit+c
380    L=L+1
390 UNTIL c=0
```

```
400 PRINT TAB(1,L+3);"Any other regular payments,"
410 PRINT TAB(1,L+4);"enter total ";
420 INPUT others
430 regular=mort+rates+rent+electric+gas+credit+others
440 CLS
450 FOR I=1 TO 25:PRINT CHR$(129):NEXT I
460 PRINT TAB(1,1)"Other outgoings this month"
470 INPUT TAB(1,4)"Outstanding bills (total) "oldbills
480 INPUT TAB(1,6)"Grocery bill "grocer
490 INPUT TAB(1,7)"Butchers bill "butcher
500 INPUT TAB(1,8)"Entertainment allowance "ents
510 b=0:L=13
520 PRINT TAB(1,12);"Other bills due this month"
530 REPEAT
540     INPUT TAB(2,L)"Amount (0 to finish) " b
550     bills=bills+b
560     L=L+1
570 UNTIL b=0
580 bills_this_month=bills+grocer+butcher+ents
590 total_out=regular+bills_this_month+oldbills
600 CLS
610 FOR I=1 TO 25:PRINT CHR$(133):NEXT I
620 PRINT TAB(1,1)"Monthly income"
630 PRINT TAB(4,3)"Your"CHR$(131)"net"CHR$(133)"income ";
640 INPUT boss
650 PRINT TAB(4,4)"Your wife's"CHR$(131)"net"CHR$(133)
            "income ";
660 INPUT wife
670 PRINT TAB(4,8)"Any other"CHR$(131)"net"CHR$(133)
            "income ";
680 INPUT more_money
690 income=boss+wife+more_money
700 balance=income-total_out
710 debit=FALSE
720 IF balance<0 THEN debit=TRUE
730 CLS
740 INPUT "Do you have a printer (Y/N)" a$
750 IF LEFT$(a$,1)="Y" OR LEFT$(a$,1)="y" THEN VDU 2
760 CLS
770 PRINT CHR$(141);CHR$(130)"          MONTHLY BUDGET"
780 PRINT CHR$(141);CHR$(130)"          MONTHLY BUDGET"
790 PRINT 'CHR$(130)"COMMENT" TAB(22);"-OUT-";TAB(33);"-IN-"
800 PRINT CHR$(130);TAB(23); "-£-"; TAB(34); "-£-"
810 PRINT ''"Regular amounts" TAB(FNP(20,regular));regular
820 PRINT '"Bills this month" TAB(FNP(20,bills_this_month));
            bills_this_month
830 PRINT '"Outstanding bills"
```

```
840 PRINT "from last month";TAB(FNP(20,oldbills));oldbills
850 PRINT '"TOTAL OUTGOINGS";TAB(FNP(20,total_out));total_out
860 PRINT ''"TOTAL INCOME";TAB(FNP(30,income));income
870 IF debit THEN position=20 ELSE position=30
880 IF debit THEN d$="DEBIT" ELSE d$="CREDIT"
890 PRINT ''d$;" BALANCE";TAB(FNP(position,balance));balance
900 VDU 3
910 @%=10
920 END
930
940 DEF FNP(column,const)
950   s=column+10-LEN(STR$(const))
960   IF const=INT(const) THEN s=s-3
970 =s
```

P34 Conversion

This is a general purpose conversion utility, which I have implemented with seventeen different conversion factors. It is fairly straightforward to choose different units to be converted by changing the data statements at the end of the program.

Seventeen conversions were chosen to make the main menu fit the screen.

Once the conversion has been chosen, the user has to decide which way the conversion has to proceed, for example, centimetres to inches or inches to centimetres.

COMMANDS

Key in program and type RUN.
Select from menu.

```
100 REM Program P34 - Conversion
110 MODE 7
120 REPEAT
130    CLS
140    PRINT "Conversion Utility" ''
150    RESTORE
160    @%=2
170    FOR I=1 TO 17
180       READ a$,b$
190       PRINT I;SPC(3);a$;" to ";b$
200    NEXT I
210    @%=10
220    PRINT
230    INPUT "Choose Option "choice
240    CLS
250    RESTORE 570
260    FOR I=1 TO choice
270       READ a$,b$
280    NEXT I
290    RESTORE 660
300    FOR I=1 TO choice
310       READ factor
320    NEXT I
330    PRINT ''"1."a$" to "b$
340    PRINT ''"2."b$" to "a$
350    INPUT '"Choose Option "choice
360    IF choice=2 THEN PROCb_to_a ELSE PROCa_to_b
```

```
370    INPUT ''"Another run? (Y/N) "res$
380 UNTIL res$<>"Y"
390 END
400
410 DEF PROCa_to_b
420    PRINT ''"Enter "a$;
430    INPUT a
440    b=a*factor
450    PRINT ''STR$(a);SPC(3);a$ " = " STR$(b);SPC(3);b$
460 ENDPROC
470
480 DEF PROCb_to_a
490    PRINT ''"Enter "b$;
500    INPUT b
510    a=b/factor
520    PRINT ''STR$(b);SPC(3);b$ " = " STR$(a);SPC(3);a$
530 ENDPROC
540
550 REM Conversions
560 REM These can be changed
570 DATA Inches,Centimetres,Feet,Metres,Yards,Metres
580 DATA Miles,Kilometres,Teaspoons,Cubic centimetres
590 DATA Tablespoons,Cubic centimetres,Cups,Litres
600 DATA Pints,Litres,Quarts,Litres,Gallons,Litres
610 DATA Ounces,Grams,Pounds,Kilograms,Tons,Kilograms
620 DATA Miles/hour,Metres/sec,Square yards,Square metres
630 DATA Years,Seconds,Atmospheres,cm Hg
640 REM Conversion data
650 REM corresponds to above
660 DATA 2.540,0.3048,0.9144,1.609,4.929,14.788,0.2366
670 DATA 0.4732,0.9463,4.546,28.3495,0.4536,907.2,0.447
680 DATA .8361,31536000,76
```

P35 Birthday List

This program uses one of the SORT routines developed later on in the book, the so-called Bubble Sort.

If you wish to see this routine operating try program P56.

The Birthday List program is used to store all those birthdays you have to remember. The program sorts the birthdays into date order, and then prints all birthdays left in the current year. All birthdays are stored in DATA statements in lines 1000 to 2000. Notice that the birthdays are terminated with EOF - end of file.

COMMANDS

Key in program, add birthdays as DATA statements then type RUN.
Follow instructions.

```
100 REM Program P35 - Birthday List
110 CLS
120 @%=2
130 PRINT "The birthdays held in this program"
140 PRINT "are held in data statements starting at"
150 PRINT "line 1000. The final data statement is"
160 PRINT "line 2000. If you wish to add more  to"
170 PRINT "the list enter the data in the format"
180 PRINT '"1100 DATA name,mmdd"'
        "where dd is day,mm is month"
190 PRINT '"Press any key"
200 Z=GET
210 CLS:I=0
220 DIM name$(100),dates(100)
230 REPEAT
240   I=I+1
250   READ name$(I),dates(I)
260 UNTIL name$(I)="EOF"
270 I=I-1
280 PROCsort
290 INPUT "What is today's date (mmdd)"date
300 PRINT '"The birthdays left this year are"'''
310 FOR J=1 TO I
320  IF dates(J)>date THEN
     PRINT name$(J);"'s birthday is ";:PROCdate
330 NEXT J
340 END
350
```

```
360 DEF PROCsort
370   FOR X=1 TO I-1
380     FOR Y=X+1 TO I
390       IF dates(Y)<dates(X) THEN PROCswap
400     NEXT Y
410   NEXT X
420 ENDPROC
430
440 DEF PROCswap
450   t=dates(Y):t$=name$(Y)
460   dates(Y)=dates(X):name$(Y)=name$(X)
470   dates(X)=t:name$(X)=t$
480 ENDPROC
490
500 DEF PROCdate
510   day=dates(J) MOD 100
520   month=dates(J) DIV 100
530   RESTORE 2000
540   FOR Z=1 TO month
550     READ m$
560   NEXT Z
570   PRINT day", "m$
580 ENDPROC
590
1000 DATA Jim Smith,1130
1010 DATA Bill Smythe,0812
1020 DATA Liz Graham,303
1030 DATA John Gordon,419
1040 DATA John Ferguson,407
1050 DATA Teresa Gordon,1222
1160 DATA EOF,0
1170
2000 DATA January,February,March,April,May,June,July,August,
        September,October,November,December,eod
```

```
What is todays date (mmdd)0116

The birthdays left this year are


Liz Graham's birthday is  3, March
John Ferguson's birthday is  7, April
John Gordon's birthday is 19, April
Bill Smythe's birthday is 12, August
Jim Smith's birthday is 30, November
Teresa Gordon's birthday is 22, December

>_
```

P36 Diary

This is one of my favourite programs. It is used to store a diary in the computer system.

The soft keys are programmed as follows:

Key 0 holds the commands   AUTO1,1 <cr>
                                      DATA

and when pressed the automatic line number utility is called in starting at line 1 and incrementing by one. Line number 1 is given the BASIC keyword DATA. Note <cr> is carriage return.

Key 1 holds the commands   <cr>
                                        DATA

and when pressed, a new BASIC program line number is generated with the BASIC keyword DATA being the first word on the line.

Key 10 – the break key, has been programmed to OLD the program memory and restart the diary program running. The program gives the user the opportunity to list the diary page on the screen.

The diary data is thus stored in the form of DATA statements. Once the diary page has been written it can be SAVEd to tape or disc as required.

COMMANDS

Key in program and type RUN.
Follow instructions as presented.
To save diary page use the following procedure;

SAVE "date"

Where "date" is the date of the diary page.

```
10000 REM Program P36 - Diary
10010 DATA "That's all"
10020 *KEY0"AUTO 1,1|MDATA"
10030 *KEY 1"|MDATA"
10040 *KEY 10"OLD|MRUN|M"
10050 MODE7
10060 PRINT CHR$(130);"KEY0";CHR$(129);"then"CHR$(130);
            "KEY1";CHR$(129);"after each line"
10070 PRINT CHR$(129);"Press "CHR$(130);"BREAK";
            CHR$(129);" to finish"
10080 VDU 28,0,24,39,4
10090 PRINT "To list diary press P"
10100  Y$=INKEY$(300)
10110 IF Y$<>"P" THEN CLS:END
10120 REPEAT
10130   READ L$
10140   PRINT L$
10150 UNTIL L$="That's all"
10160 END
```

P37, P38, and P39 Christmas Card List System

As an example of a home records management system, I have included these three programs which are used to organise our Christmas card list.

The same outline programs could be used to hold club records, records of various collections, or indeed kitchen stock records.

The system will run on a model A, but print program requires a printer to print out the Christmas Print List.

The system diagram is as follows:

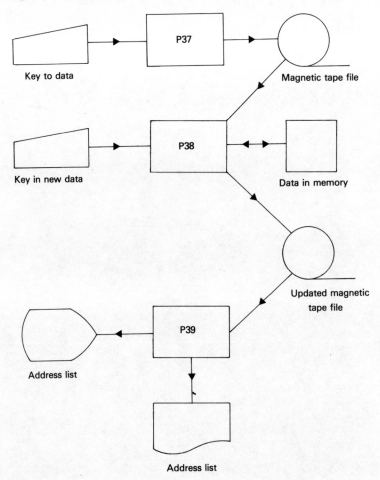

Key to data

P37

Magnetic tape file

Key in new data

P38

Data in memory

Updated magnetic tape file

Address list

P39

Address list

COMMANDS

Ensure that tape recorder and printer are ready.
Key in program(s), and type RUN.
Follow instructions.

```
100 REM Program P37 - Christmas Card List Creation
110 MODE7
120 PRINT "Place data tape in recorder and rewind"
130 PRINT '"Press any key when ready"
140 X=GET
150 INPUT ''"What is the name of datafile ",f$
160 f_no=OPENOUT(f$)
170 REPEAT
180    INPUT "Name - (last to finish)"name$
190    IF name$="last" THEN 290
200    INPUT "Address 1 - "address_1$
210    INPUT "Address 2 - "address_2$
220    INPUT "Address 3 - "address_3$
230    INPUT "Post_code - "post_code$
240    INPUT '''"Last post date - "date$
250    PRINT '''
260    PRINT#f_no,name$,address_1$,address_2$,address_3$,
                  post_code$,date$
270    X=INKEY(100)
280    CLS
290 UNTIL name$="last"
300 CLOSE #f_no
310 END


100 REM Program P38 - Christmas Card List Maintenance
110 DIM line$(200)
120 MODE7
130 job_done=FALSE
140 REPEAT
150  CLS
160  PRINT '''''"  C H R I S T M A S    C A R D"
170  PRINT '''" L I S T   M A I N T E N A N C E "
180  PRINT '''
190  PRINT " 1. Add a new name"
200  PRINT " 2. Remove a name"
210  PRINT " 3. END"
220  PRINT ''
230
240  INPUT "Enter appropriate code for job " selection
250  ON selection GOSUB 280,420:ELSE job_done=TRUE
260 UNTIL job_done
270 END
```

```
280
290 REM Add a new name routine
300 PROCread_list
310 CLS
320 INPUT "New name",name$
330 INPUT "Address_1",address_1$
340 INPUT "Address_2",address_2$
350 INPUT "Address_3",address_3$
360 INPUT "Post Code",post_code$
370 INPUT "Last post date",date$
380 no_of_entries=no_of_entries+1
390 line$(no_of_entries)=name$+","+address_1$+","+address_2$+
                      ","+address_3$+","+post_code$+","+date$
400 PROCwrite_list
410 RETURN
420
430 REM Remove a name
440 PROCread_list
450 CLS
460 INPUT '"Which name has to be removed ",old_name$
470 I=0
480 flag=FALSE
490 REPEAT
500  I=I+1
510  IF LEFT$(line$(I),INSTR(line$(I),",")-1) = old_name$
     THEN flag=TRUE
520 UNTIL flag=TRUE
530 FOR J=I TO no_of_entries-1
540  line$(J)=line$(J+1)
550 NEXT J
560 no_of_entries=no_of_entries-1
570 PROCwrite_list
580 RETURN
590
600 DEF PROCread_list
610 CLS
620 INPUT '"" What is the name of the Christmas card file " f$
630 PRINT '"""Place data file cassette in recorder and"
640 PRINT "wind to correct position. Press any key"
650 PRINT "when ready"
660 x=GET
670 PRINT "Press PLAY button"
680 f_no=OPENIN(f$)
690 I=0
```

```
700 REPEAT
710   I=I+1
720   INPUT#f_no,name$,address_1$,address_2$,address_3$,
               post_code$,date$
730   line$(I)=name$+","+address_1$+","+address_2$+",
               "+address_3$+","+post_code$+","+date$
740 UNTIL EOF#f_no
750 CLOSE #f_no
760 no_of_entries=I
770 ENDPROC
780
790 DEF PROCwrite_list
800 CLS
810 INPUT''"What is the name of the new Christmas"'
          "card file "f$
820 PRINT ''"Place cassette in recorder. Press any"
830 PRINT "key when ready"
840 X=GET
850 f_no=OPENOUT(f$)
860 I=0
870 REPEAT
880 I=I+1
890   name$=FNstrip(I)
900   address_1$=FNstrip(I)
910   address_2$=FNstrip(I)
920   address_3$=FNstrip(I)
930   post_code$=FNstrip(I)
940   date$=line$(I)
950   PRINT#f_no,name$,address_1$,address_2$,address_3$,
            post_code$,date$
960 UNTIL I=no_of_entries
970 CLOSE#f_no
980 ENDPROC
990
1000 DEF FNstrip(I)
1010   temp=INSTR(line$(I),",")
1020   l$=LEFT$(line$(I),temp-1)
1030   line$(I)=RIGHT$(line$(I),LEN(line$(I))-temp)
1040=l$
```

```
100 REM Program P39 - Christmas Card List Print
110 MODE7
120 PRINT "Place data tape in recorder and rewind"
130 PRINT '"Press any key when ready"
140 X=GET
150 PRINT ''"Make sure that printer is ready and"
160 PRINT "paper is aligned properly"
170 PRINT '"Press any key when ready"
180 X=GET
190 REM PLACE CODE TO SELECT YOUR PRINTER HERE
200 INPUT ''"What is the name of datafile ",f$
210 PRINT "Press PLAY"
220 f_no=OPENIN(f$)
230 VDU 2 :REM enable printer
240 REPEAT
250     INPUT#f_no,name$,address_1$,address_2$,
                    address_3$,post_code$,date$
260     PRINT name$
270     PRINT address_1$
280     PRINT address_2$
290     PRINT address_3$
300     PRINT post_code$
310     PRINT '''
320     PRINT date$
330 UNTIL EOF#f_no
340 CLOSE #f_no
350 VDU 3 :REM disable printer
360 END
```

P40 Calendar

This program can be used to print out the calendar for any month in the twentieth century. The program is based on an idea of my father-in-law, John Campbell.

Note that month must be in the correct format eg. March, April. If you wish to make the program more insensitive to data input then see the routines in P41.

COMMANDS

Key in program and type RUN.
Enter month when requested.

```
100 REM Program P40 - Calendar
110 DIM day_name$(7),calendar$(7,6)
120 FOR I=1 TO 7:READ day_name$(I):NEXT I
130 MODE7
140 PRINT TAB(12,12) "C A L E N D A R"
150 Z=INKEY(300)
160 CLS
170 INPUT''"Which month do you require (eg January)?"
        ' month$
180 REPEAT
190     READ m$,first_of_the_month,days_in_month
200     month=month+1
210 UNTIL month$=m$
220 INPUT ''"Which year do you require? "year
230 IF year>1900 THEN year=year-1900
240 no_of_leap_years=year DIV 4
250 this_is_leap_year=FALSE
260 IF year MOD 4=0 THEN this_is_leap_year=TRUE
270 offset=year+no_of_leap_years
280 IF this_is_leap_year AND month<3 THEN offset=offset-1
290 IF this_is_leap_year AND month=2 THEN days_in_month=29
300 offset=offset MOD 7
310 first_of_the_month=(first_of_the_month + offset) MOD 7
320 IF first_of_the_month=0 THEN first_of_the_month=7
330 FOR I=1 TO first_of_the_month - 1
340     calendar$(I,1)=" "
350 NEXT I
360 day=1
370 FOR I=first_of_the_month TO 7
380     calendar$(I,1)=STR$(day)
390     day=day+1
400 NEXT I
```

```
410
420 FOR J=2 TO 6
430   FOR I=1 TO 7
440     calendar$(I,J)=STR$(day)
450     day=day+1
460     IF day>days_in_month THEN I=7:J=6
470   NEXT I
480 NEXT J
490 CLS
500 PRINT TAB(10,3);month$,year+1900
510 FOR I=1 TO 7
520   PRINT TAB(5,I+10);day_name$(I);
530 NEXT I
540 FOR J=1 TO 6
550   FOR I=1 TO 7
560     PRINT TAB(J*3+10,I+10);calendar$(I,J);
570   NEXT I
580 NEXT J
590 PRINT
600 END
610
620 DATA Mon,Tue,Wed,Thu,Fri,Sat,Sun
630 DATA January,1,31,February,4,28,March,4,31,April,7,30
640 DATA May,2,31,June,5,30,July,7,31,August,3,31,September,6,30
650 DATA October,1,31,November,4,30,December,6,31
```

March 1983

```
Mon           7  14  21  28
Tue       1   8  15  22  29
Wed       2   9  16  23  30
Thu       3  10  17  24  31
Fri       4  11  18  25
Sat       5  12  19  26
Sun       6  13  20  27
```

P41 Telephone List

This program allows the user to select a telephone number from a list held as DATA statements.

You do not have to enter the full name to select the number. As long as the string entered is part of one of the names, then the telephone number is displayed.
Note the use of FNcase which turns lower case characters into upper case. This routine could be used to improve some of the other programs. The data names used within the routine are all LOCAL.

COMMANDS

Key in program.
Enter telephone list as DATA statements before line 340.
Type RUN.
Enter name when requested.

```
100 REM Program P41 - Telephone List
110 CLS
120 PRINT TAB(10,4)  "Telephone Directory"
130 REPEAT
140    RESTORE
150    count=0
160    PRINT ''"Whose number do you want?";
170    REPEAT
180      INPUT name$
190    UNTIL   name$<>""
200    CLS
210    name$=FNcase(name$)
220    REPEAT
230      READ  entry$,number$
240      IF INSTR(entry$,name$)>0 THEN PRINT entry$
         "'s number is "number$:count=count+1
250    UNTIL   entry$="EOF"
260    IF count=0 THEN
       PRINT "We have no number corresponding to  "name$
270    INPUT ''"Another number",answer$
280    a$=LEFT$(answer$,1)
290 UNTIL a$="n" OR a$="N"
300 END
310
320 DEF FNcase(a$)
330    LOCAL d$,I,c$,c
340    d$=""
```

```
350    FOR I=1 TO LEN(a$)
360      c$=MID$(a$,I,1)
370      c=ASC(c$)
380      IF c>96 AND c<122 THEN c$=CHR$(c-32)
390      d$=d$+c$
400    NEXT I
410= d$
420
430 REM Place your telephone numbers on the following lines
440 DATA BILL SMITH,12345,BILL JONES,45678,
            ALICE GRAHAM,01-234 6542
450 DATA FRANCIS CAMPBELL,EK 24316,JOHN GORDON,EK 49400
460 DATA EOF,EOF
```

P42 Investments

This program calculates how much income can be generated from capital if the interest earned by that capital is known.

The user is presented with the choice of increasing his or her income at the expense of reducing capital. Not having any capital, I have not yet had recourse to using the program, but it's nice to dream!

COMMANDS

Key in program and type RUN.

```
100 REM Program P42   - Investments
110 MODE 7
120 @%=&2020A
130 PRINT "This program allows the user to plan"
140 PRINT "his future investments, given that he"
150 PRINT "wishes his investment to give him a"
160 PRINT "regular income"
170 INPUT ''"Income required (montnly) £"income
180 INPUT "Interest rate (% per annum) "interest
190 interest=interest/100
200 REM assume that investment interest is compounded
        monthly
210 investment=income*12/interest
220 PRINT ''"An investment of "'"£";investment'
        "will provide a monthly income of"'"£"; income
230 PRINT '"Note tnat no capital is used."'
240 PRINT "If you wish to use up your capital how"
250 PRINT "many years do you require an income for"
260 INPUT years
270 interest=interest/12
280 temp=(1+interest)^(12*years)
290 investment=income*(temp-1)/interest/temp
300 PRINT ''"An investment of £";investment'
        "will provide a montnly income of"'"£";
        income '"for "STR$(years)" years"
310 END
```

P43 Circles

It takes a minute or so for this program to finish, but I think that the effect is quite pretty.

The program draws two sets of concentric circles, with colour changing from circle to circle. This is done in lines 130-170.

The routine for drawing the circle is given in PROC circle.

Once the cirles are drawn out, the colours of the circles are quickly changed to give the impression of motion.

COMMANDS

Key in program and type RUN.

```
100 REM    Program P43 - Circles
110 CLS
120 PRINT TAB(10,10)"SETTING UP .";
130 DIM sinp(63),cosp(63)
140 FOR I%=1 TO 63
150    sinp(I%)=SIN(I%*.1)
160    cosp(I%)=COS(I%*.1)
170    PRINT ".";
180 NEXT I%
190 MODE 5
200 VDU 5
210 FOR Y = 10 TO 1000   STEP 25
220    GCOL 0, Y MOD 3 +1
230    PROCcircle(Y,1)
240    PROCcircle(Y,2)
250 NEXT Y
260 K=0
270 REPEAT
280    FOR I=1 TO 3
290    VDU 19,I,(I+K) MOD 3+5;0;
300    NEXT I
310    K=(K+1) MOD 5 +1
320    FOR I=1 TO 80:NEXT I
330 UNTIL 0
340 END
```

```
350 DEF PROCcircle(R,C)
360    IF C=1 THEN VDU 29,428;512; ELSE VDU 29,856;512;
370    P=0:MOVE0,R
380    FOR I%=1 TO 63
390       DRAW R*sinp(I%),R*cosp(I%)
400    NEXT I%
410 ENDPROC
```

P44 Interference

This program generates an interference type pattern.

Once the pattern has been generated, the user can redefine the colours by pressing any key.

COMMANDS

Key in program and type RUN.
When pattern is generated press any key to change colours.

```
100 REM Program P44 - Interference
110 MODE 5
120 VDU 5
130 FOR Y=0 TO 1023 STEP 4
140   GCOL 3,Y MOD 3
150   MOVE 0,Y
160   DRAW 1279,1023-Y
170 NEXT Y
180 FOR X=1279 TO 0 STEP -8
190   GCOL 3,X MOD 3
200   MOVE X,0
210   DRAW 1279-X,1023
220 NEXT X
230
240 REPEAT
250   B=GET
260   FOR C=0 TO 3
270     VDU 19,C,RND(8)-1;0;
280   NEXT C
290 UNTIL 0
```

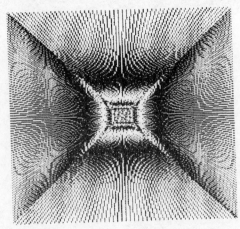

P45 Picture

This program is used just to produce a pretty picture on the screen.

COMMANDS

Key in program and type RUN.

```
100 REM Program P45 - Picture
110 REPEAT
120    MODE 5
130    VDU 5
140    COL=1:SHADE=RND(8)
150    VDU 29,640;512;
160    MOVE 0,0
170    FOR A%=0 TO 500
180       GCOL 3,A% MOD 3 + 1
190       DRAW 800*SIN(A%/20),800*COS(A%/20)
200       MOVE 0,0
210       FOR J%=1 TO 3
220          VDU 19,J%,(COL+J%) MOD 3 + SHADE;0;
230       NEXT J%
240       COL=(COL+1) MOD 3
250    NEXT A%
260 UNTIL 0
```

P46 Pictures

This is a rather crude graphics editor. The program allows the user to draw squares, circles, triangles and lines on the screen.

The screen uses a text window at the bottom of the screen to allow the user to enter their picture elements.

The different parts of the picture are accessed via the function keys. It helps if a slip of paper is inserted under the clear plastic strip with the functions written on it.

When a picture element is drawn, the user has the opportunity of undrawing it. Other commands could be designed as required.

COMMANDS

Key in program and type RUN.
            Press key 0 for square.
                  key 1 for circle.
                  key 2 for triangle.
                  key 3 for line.
                  key 4 for end of program.

```
100 REM Program P46 - Pictures
110 MODE 7
120 REM set up arrays for circle
130 DIM sinp(63),cosp(63)
140 FOR I%=0 TO 63
150   sinp(I%)=SIN(I%*.1):cosp(I%)=COS(I%*.1)
160 NEXT I%
170 PRINT "Use the program to develop pictures,"
180 PRINT "the basic shapes that you have are:"
190 PRINT "square,circle,triangle,and line."
200 PRINT '"The program uses mode 5, you have 4"
210 PRINT "colours to choose from"
220 PRINT ''
230 INPUT "Background (0 to 15)" bgrnd%
240 INPUT "Foreground 1 colour" f1
250 INPUT "Foreground 2 colour" f2
260 INPUT "Foreground 3 colour" f3
270 PRINT ''"The function keys are programmed for"
280 PRINT "the shapes f0=square,f1=circle"
290 PRINT "f2=triangle,and f3=line"
300 PRINT "f4=END"
```

```
310 PRINT ''"Press any key to start"
320 Z=GET
330 MODE 5
340 VDU 19,0,bgrnd%;0;
350 VDU 19,1,f1;0;
360 VDU 19,2,f2;0;
370 VDU 19,3,f3;0;
380 *KEY0"1"
390 *KEY1"2"
400 *KEY2"3"
410 *KEY3"4"
420 *KEY4"5"
430 REPEAT
440   VDU 28,0,31,19,31
450   X=GET:X=X-48
460   ON X GOSUB 500,700,950,1160 ELSE VDU12
470 UNTIL X=5
480 END
490
500 REM Square
510 PRINT "SQUARE";
520 Z=INKEY(100)
530 INPUT '"X-COORD" X "Y-COORD" Y "SIDE" S
540 INPUT "COLOUR" C
550
560 FOR I=1 TO 2
570   GCOL 0,C
580   MOVE X,Y
590   MOVE X+S,Y
600   PLOT 85,X+S,Y-S
610   MOVE X,Y
620   PLOT 85,X,Y-S
630   IF I=1 INPUT "Square ok" a$
640   q=LEFT$(a$,1)="Y" OR LEFT$(a$,1)="y"
650   IF NOT q THEN C=0 ELSE I=2
660 NEXT I
670 PRINT
680 RETURN
690
700 REM Circle
710 PRINT "Circle";
720 Z=INKEY(200)
730 INPUT '"X-CENTRE" X "Y-CENTRE" Y "RADIUS" R
740 INPUT "COLOUR" C
750 VDU 29,X;Y;
760
770 FOR I=1 TO 2
780   GCOL 0,C
```

```
790    MOVE 0,R
800
810    FOR P%=0 TO 63
820      MOVE 0,0
830      PLOT 85,R*sinp(P%),R*cosp(P%)
840    NEXT P%
850
860    IF I=1 INPUT "Circle ok" a$
870    q=LEFT$(a$,1)="Y" OR LEFT$(a$,1)="y"
880    IF NOT q THEN C=0 ELSE I=2
890  NEXT I
900
910  VDU 29,0;0;
920  PRINT
930  RETURN
940
950  REM Triangle
960  PRINT "Triangle";
970  Z=INKEY(200)
980  INPUT '"X1= " X1 "Y1= " Y1
990  INPUT "X2= " X2 "Y2= " Y2
1000 INPUT "X3= " X3 "Y3= " Y3
1010 INPUT "Colour " C
1020
1030 FOR I=1 TO 2
1040   GCOL 0,C
1050   MOVE X1,Y1
1060   MOVE X2,Y2
1070   PLOT 85,X3,Y3
1080   IF I=1 INPUT "Triangle ok" a$
1090   q=LEFT$(a$,1)="Y" OR LEFT$(a$,1)="y"
1100   IF NOT q THEN C=0 ELSE I=2
1110 NEXT I
1120
1130 PRINT
1140 RETURN
1150
1160 REM Line
1170 PRINT "Line";
1180 Z=INKEY(200)
1190 INPUT '"X1= " X1 "Y1= " Y1
1200 INPUT "X2= " X2 "Y2= " Y2
1210 INPUT "Colour " C
1220
1230 FOR I=1 TO 2
1240   GCOL 0,C
1250   MOVE X1,Y1
1260   DRAW X2,Y2
```

```
1270    IF I=1 INPUT "Line ok" a$
1280    q=LEFT$(a$,1)="Y" OR LEFT$(a$,1)="y"
1290    IF NOT q THEN C=0 ELSE I=2
1300 NEXT I
1310
1320 PRINT
1330 RETURN
```

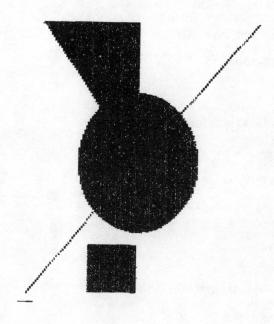

P47 Zoom

One way of zooming in or out of a picture is to redraw the whole scene to a different size.

This program draws a cube and allows the user to zoom the cube into and out of the screen.

COMMANDS

Key in program and type RUN.
Press key I to zoom in.
Press key O to zoom out.

```
100 REM Program 47 - Zoom
110 MODE 4
120 S=200
130 colour=1
140 not_colour=0
150 count=0
160 VDU 19,0,4;0;19,1,3;0;
170 VDU 29,640;512;
180 GCOL 0,1
190 PROCcube(S)
200 REPEAT
210   REPEAT
220     DS=INKEY(-38) - INKEY(-55)
230     DS=DS*10
240   UNTIL DS<>0
250   GCOL 0,not_colour
260   PROCcube(S)
270   GCOL 0,colour
280   PROCcube(S+DS)
290   S=S+DS
300 UNTIL 0
301
310 DEF PROCcube(S)
320 IF S<0 THEN ENDPROC
330   MOVE -S,S
340   DRAW S,S
350   DRAW S,-S
360   DRAW S+S/2,0
370   DRAW S+S/2,2*S
380   DRAW S/2-S,2*S
390   DRAW -S,S
```

```
400   DRAW -S,-S
410   DRAW S,-S
420   MOVE S,S
430   DRAW S+S/2,2*S
440   ENDPROC
```

P48 Worm

I like this program: it is used as an example of motion.
When the program is RUNning a little worm slithers across
the screen. The motion is fairly smooth since the next worm
to be plotted is drawn in background first, and then colours
are changed to shift from one position to the next.

COMMANDS

Key in program and type RUN.

```
100 REM Program 48 - Worm
110 MODE 5
120 S=0
130 count=0
140 colour=RND(7)
150 VDU 29,0;512;
160 VDU 19,3,colour;0;:REM Foreground=colour
170 VDU 19,1,colour;0;:REM Drawing colour=colour
180 VDU 5
190 GCOL 0,1
200 PROCstraight(S)
210 DS=50
220 REPEAT
230   REPEAT
240     S=S+DS
250     count=count+1
260     plot_colour=count MOD 2 + 1
270     GCOL 1,plot_colour
280     PROCbent(S)
290     VDU 19,plot_colour,colour;0;
300     VDU 19,3-plot_colour,0;0;
310     GCOL 2,plot_colour
320     PROCstraight(S-DS)
330 REM do again moving worm
340 Z=INKEY(10):REM slow it down
350     S=S+DS
360     count=count+1
370     plot_colour=count MOD 2 + 1
380     GCOL 1,plot_colour
390     PROCstraight(S)
400     VDU 19,plot_colour,colour;0;
410     VDU 19,3-plot_colour,0;0;
420     GCOL 2,plot_colour
430     PROCbent(S-DS)
440   UNTIL S>1280 OR S<0
```

```
450    DS=-DS
460 UNTIL 0
470 END
480
490 DEF PROCstraight(S)
500    MOVE S,0
510    DRAW S+100,0
520 ENDPROC
530
540 DEF PROCbent(S)
550    MOVE S,0
560    DRAW S+20,0
570    DRAW S+40,20
580    DRAW S+60,0
590    DRAW S+100,0
600 ENDPROC
```

P49 Drawing

This program allows the user to doodle on the screen.

COMMANDS

Key in program and type RUN.

Press key "W" to draw in white.
"B" to draw in black.
"C" to clear the screen.

Use cursor control keys to draw.

```
100 REM Program P49 - Drawing
110 MODE 4
120 VDU 5
130 MOVE 639,511
140 REPEAT
150    IF INKEY(-83) THEN CLS:MOVE 639,511
160    IF INKEY(-101) THEN GCOL 0,0
170    IF INKEY(-34) THEN GCOL 0,1
180    X=INKEY(-26) - INKEY(-122)
190    Y=INKEY (-42) - INKEY(-58)
200    PLOT 1,X,Y
210 UNTIL 0
```

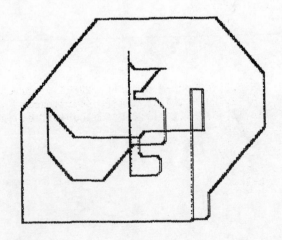

P50 MODE 7 Colours

It is possible to write chunky graphics in various colours in MODE 7. Some of the games were in fact written in MODE 7.

This program shows the different colours available. The first title for this program was "see your name in lights"

COMMANDS

Key in program and type RUN.
Press key to get next colour.

```
100 REM Program P50 - MODE 7 COLOURS
110 MODE7
120 @%=3
130 PRINT TAB(12,12)"M O D E  7"
140 PRINT TAB(11,15)"C O L O U R S"
150 Z=INKEY(300)
160 CLS
170 PRINT '"This program shows the range of "
180 PRINT "colours available in MODE 7."
190 PRINT '"The program prompts you for your name,"
200 PRINT "the name is then written double size "
210 PRINT "in the various MODE 7 colours. To see"
220 PRINT "the next colour press any key."
230 PRINT '"Press any key to continue"
240 Z=GET
250 INPUT '''"Name- "name$
260 CLS
270 offset=0
280 REPEAT
290   colour=129
300   REPEAT
310     PRINT TAB(0,0)"COLOUR="colour"  OFFSET ="offset;
320     PRINT TAB(12,12)CHR$(141);CHR$(colour);name$
330     PRINT TAB(12,13)CHR$(141);CHR$(colour+offset);name$
340     colour = colour+1
350     Z=GET
360   UNTIL colour=152
370   offset=offset+1
380 UNTIL offset=4
```

P51 Writing Text At The Graphics Cursor

This is a demonstration program showing the use of various coloured text, and also showing how the text and graphics cursors can be combined to produce interesting effects, such as writing along a sine or cosine curve.

Try the effect of other functions in line 370 and 390.

COMMANDS

Key in and type RUN

```
100 REM Program P51 - Writing Text at the Graphics Cursor
110 MODE 5
120 VDU 19,0,2;0;19,3,4;0;19,2,5;0;
130 COLOUR 1
140 PRINT '"This program shows"
150 PRINT '"the interesting"
160 PRINT '"effect of writing"
170 PRINT '"text at the"
180 PRINT '"graphics cursor."
190 COLOUR 2
200 PRINT ''"The program writes"
210 PRINT '"text in various"
220 PRINT '"colours."
230 COLOUR 3
240 PRINT ''"Superimposed on"
250 PRINT '"the text are"
260 PRINT '"simple mathematical"
270 PRINT '"functions."
280 COLOUR 1
290 PRINT '''"H O W Z A T !!!"
300
310 REM and now writing at graphics
320 sin$="SIN ":cos$="COS "
330 VDU 5:REM write text at graphics
340 X=0:K=0
350 GCOL 4,0
360 REPEAT
370    MOVE X,SIN(-PI+X*2*PI/1280)*200+800
380    PRINT MID$(sin$,K+1,1)
390    MOVE X,COS(-PI+X*2*PI/1280)*200+300
400    PRINT MID$(cos$,K+1,1)
```

```
410
420   X=X+40
430   K=((K+1) MOD 4)
440   UNTIL X>1278
```

This program shows
the interesting
effect of writing
text at the
graphics cursor.

The program writes
text in various
colours.

Superimposed on
the text are
simple mathematical
functions

WOW ZAT !!!
>

P52 Screen Dump   MODEL B ONLY

I have used two methods of obtaining a copy of the screen
onto paper.

    1. Using a Video Printer.
    2. Dump the screen to a printer or plotter.

This program was written to dump the screen to the CALCOMP
flat bed plotter. The CALCOMP is a rather expensive machine,
but the structure of the program could be adapted to any
printer or plotter which can be driven from software.

COMMANDS

Set up plotter or printer, key in program.
Amend program to fit your own printer/plotter.
Type in graphics program, using line numbers below 100.
Type RUN.

```
 10 MODE 5
 20 GCOL 0,1
 30 MOVE 0,100:MOVE 0,0:PLOT 85,100,100
 40 MOVE 500,500:GCOL 0,2:PLOT 85,0,1000
 50 VDU 29,800;800;
 60 GCOL 0,3
 70 MOVE 0,80
 80 FOR P=0 TO PI*2 STEP .01:MOVE 0,0:
    PLOT 85,80*SIN(P),80*COS(P):NEXT P
 90 VDU 29,0;0;
100 REM Program P52 - Screen Dump
110 REM Parameters to change are:
120 REM    no_of_colours
130 REM    step_size_x
140 REM    step_size_y
150 REM
160 REM Set pens in CALCOMP to correct colours
170 REM Select paper to be same colour as graphic background
180 REM MODE is selected by Graphics Program
190 *FX5,2
200 *FX8,5
210 VDU 2
220 VDU 21:REM Disable VDU drivers
230 no_of_colours=3
240 step_size_x=1280/160
250 step_size_y=1024/256
```

```
260 REM The above configures the program for MODE 5
270 FOR colour=1 TO no_of_colours
280  PROCselect(colour)
290  PROChome
300  FOR X=0 TO 1279 STEP step_size_x
310   FOR Y=0 TO 1023 STEP step_size_y
320    IF POINT(X,Y)=colour THEN PROCplot(X,Y)
330   NEXT Y
340  NEXT X
350 NEXT colour
360 END
370
380 DEF PROCselect(colour)
390  PRINT "F0"
400  PRINT "F"colour
410 ENDPROC
420
430 DEF PROChome
440  PRINT"H";
450  PRINT "0/OK"
460 ENDPROC
470
480 DEF PROCplot(X,Y)
490  X%=(X DIV step_size_x)*10
500  Y%=(Y DIV step_size_y)*10
510  PRINT "H";
520  PRINT X%"/"Y%"K"
530  PRINT "I";
540  PRINT X%+1"/"Y%"K"
550 ENDPROC
```

P53 Pie Chart

This is a fairly self explanatory program which can be used
to produce a pie chart on the screen.

To speed up the initial display of the chart, I have
included a parameter "res" to indicate the resolution of the
pie chart. If res is large, 0.2, say, the resulting chart
may not be very accurate. Therefore once the chart has been
drawn there is the option of refining the picture.

It would also be interesting to plot the data on the screen.
That is left as an exercise for the reader.

COMMANDS

Key in program and type RUN.
Enter data as requested.

```
100 REM Program P53 - Pie Chart
110 DIM item(20)
120 MODE 7
130
140 PRINT CHR$(131);CHR$(141);
        "This program depicts a pie chart based";
150 PRINT CHR$(131);CHR$(141);
        "This program depicts a pie chart based"
160 PRINT CHR$(131);CHR$(141);
        "on data which you enter, one at a time";
170 PRINT CHR$(131);CHR$(141);
        "on data which you enter, one at a time"
180 PRINT CHR$(131);CHR$(141);
        "Different areas of the pie chart are"
190 PRINT CHR$(131);CHR$(141);
        "Different areas of the pie chart are"
200 PRINT 'CHR$(131);CHR$(141);
        "painted in different colours, thus we"
210 PRINT CHR$(131);CHR$(141);
        "painted in different colours, thus we"
220 PRINT 'CHR$(131);CHR$(141);
        "will plot the data in MODE 5"
230 PRINT CHR$(131);CHR$(141);
        "will plot the data in MODE 5"
240
250 PRINT '''"Enter the data one item at a time"
260 PRINT "Enter 0 to finish"
270
280 I=0
```

```
290 REPEAT
300     I=I+1
310     INPUT item(I)
320     total=total+item(I)
330     PRINT CHR$(11);SPC(40);CHR$(11);
340 REM CHR$(11)=up
350 UNTIL item(I)=0
360 INPUT "Resolution in radians",res
370
380 REPEAT
390   MODE 5
400   VDU 19,0,7;0;19,3,4;0;
410   PRINT ''SPC(5);"Pie CHART"
420
430   IF (I-1) MOD 3 =1 THEN flag=-1 ELSE flag=0
440   IF flag=-1 THEN last_item=I-2 ELSE last_item=I-1
450
460   last_angle=0:angle=0
470   MOVE 639,511:MOVE 1039,511
480
490   FOR J=1 TO last_item
500       GCOL 0,(J MOD 3)+1
510       PROCsegment
520       last_angle=last_angle+2*PI*item(J)/total
530   NEXT J
540
550   IF flag=-1 THEN  GCOL0,3:PROCsegment
560   PRINT TAB(0,30);"New resolution (Y/N)";
570   INPUT ans$
580   IF ans$="Y" OR ans$="y" THEN
    INPUT "Resolution",res:again=-1 ELSE again=0
590 UNTIL NOT again
600 END
610
620
630 DEF PROCsegment
640   REPEAT
650       MOVE 639,511
660       PLOT 85,400*COS(angle)+639,400*SIN(angle)+511
670       angle=angle+res
680       PLOT 85,400*COS(angle)+639,400*SIN(angle)+511
690       angle=angle+res
700   UNTIL angle>last_angle+2*PI*item(J)/total
710 ENDPROC
```

P54 Bar Chart

This program can draw a chart of up to thirty bars onto the screen. The bars are automatically scaled to fit onto the screen. The chart is not labelled. This is left as an exercise for the reader.

COMMANDS

Key in program and type RUN.
Enter number of bars, less than 30.
Enter the value of each bar as requested.

```
100 REM Program P54 - Bar Chart
110 MODE 7
120 @%=3
130 INPUT "Enter number of bars (<30) "bars
140 DIM val(bars)
150 max=0
160 FOR I= 1 TO bars
170   INPUT "Value of bar " val(I)
180   IF val(I)>max THEN max = val(I)
190 NEXT I
200
210 CLS
220 scale=1
230 IF max>20 THEN scale=max / 20
240
250 FOR I=1 TO bars
260   val(I)=INT(val(I)/scale)
270 NEXT I
280
290 FOR I=1 TO 20 STEP 2
300   PRINT TAB(0,22-I) INT(I*scale);
310 NEXT I
320
330 FOR I=0 TO 22
340   PRINT TAB(4,I)CHR$(146);CHR$(234);
350 NEXT I
360
370
380 FOR I=1 TO bars+1
390   PRINT TAB(5+I,22)CHR$(240);
400 NEXT I
410
```

```
420 FOR I=1 TO bars
430   FOR J=1 TO val(I)
440     PRINT TAB(6+I,22-J) CHR$(234);
450   NEXT J
460 NEXT I
470 PRINT TAB(0,23) ""
480 Z=GET
```

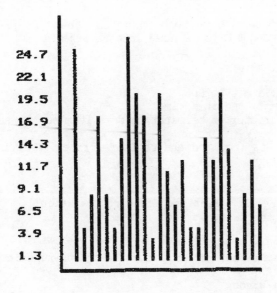

P55 Mean and Standard Deviation

This program written in MODE 7, with some error-correcting routines, is used to find the mean and standard deviation of a list of data items. If the user has a printer, then a printout of the results can be obtained.

Notice that the data are stored in the form of a string, therefore as the program stands it will only handle a limited number of data items.

If more data items have to be handled, then the program should be amended to change num$ into an array.

COMMANDS

Key in program and type RUN.
Enter data items, one at a time.
Make first character of terminating data item non-numeric to finish.
If a printer, is required ensure that correct *FX commands have been entered.

```
100 REM Program P55 - Mean and Standard Deviation
110 REM Using the teletext mode - MODE 7
120 MODE 7
130 ON ERROR RUN:
    REM catches effect of first item being non-numeric
140 PROCsetup
150 REM define window
160 P$=CHR$(141)+CHR$(131)+CHR$(157)+CHR$(129)
170 PRINT P$;"This program can be used to"
180 PRINT P$;"This program can be used to"
190 PRINT P$;"calculate the mean and standard"
200 PRINT P$;"calculate the mean and standard"
210 PRINT P$;"deviation of a set of ";CHR$(133);"numeric"
220 PRINT P$;"deviation of a set of ";CHR$(133);"numeric"
230 PRINT P$;"data. Enter your data one item"
240 PRINT P$;"data. Enter your data one item"
250 PRINT P$;"at a time, terminating "
260 PRINT P$;"at a time, terminating "
270 PRINT P$;"the data with any ";CHR$(133);"non-numeric"
280 PRINT P$;"the data with any ";CHR$(133);"non-numeric"
290 PRINT P$;"character"
300 PRINT P$;"character"
310 PRINT''
320
```

```
330 Q$=CHR$(141)+CHR$(131)+CHR$(157)+CHR$(133)
340 REPEAT
350   PRINT TAB(10,20)Q$;"Next item ";SPC(16);
360   PRINT TAB(10,21)Q$;"Next item ";SPC(16);
370   PROCgetnumb
380   IF NOT end THEN PROCcalcs
390 UNTIL end
400
410
420 REM calculate and output results
430 CLS
440 mean=total/no_of_numbers
450 deviation=SQR(sum_of_squares/no_of_numbers-mean*mean)
460 PRINT P$;"The mean of the data is  "
470 PRINT P$;"The mean of the data is  "
480 PRINT P$;mean
490 PRINT P$;mean
500 PRINT CHR$(141);CHR$(131);CHR$(157)
510 PRINT CHR$(141);CHR$(131);CHR$(157)
520 PRINT P$;"And the standard deviation is"
530 PRINT P$;"And the standard deviation is"
540 PRINT P$;deviation
550 PRINT P$;deviation
560 PRINT CHR$(141);CHR$(131);CHR$(157)
570 PRINT CHR$(141);CHR$(131);CHR$(157)
580 PRINT P$;"Do you want a print-out(Y/N)?"
590 PRINT P$;"Do you want a print-out(Y/N)?"
600 FOR I=1 TO 10
610   PRINT CHR$(141);CHR$(131);CHR$(157)
620 NEXT I
630 REPEAT ans$=GET$:UNTIL ASC(ans$)<>13
640 IF NOT( ans$="Y" OR ans$="y") THEN END
650 PRINT CHR$(2):REM enable printer
660 CLS
670 PRINT " "
680 PRINT " "
690 PRINT "The data were: "
700 PRINT " "
710 PRINT LEFT$(numb$,LEN(numb$)-1)
720 PRINT " "
730 PRINT "The mean is "mean
740 PRINT " "
750 PRINT "The standard deviation is "deviation
760 PRINT CHR$(3): REM disable printer
770
780 END
790 REM The procedures
800
```

```
 810 DEF PROCgetnumb
 820   LOCAL B$,I,K
 830   K=0
 840   REPEAT B$=GET$: UNTIL ASC(B$)<>13
 850   PRINT TAB(25,20);B$:PRINT TAB(25,21);B$
 860   IF FNcheck(B$) end=-1: ENDPROC
 870   A$=B$
 880   FOR I=1 TO 14:REM max no of digits=14
 890
 900     REPEAT
 910        B$=GET$
 920        IF B$="." THEN K=K+1
 930        B=VAL(B$)=0 AND NOT(B$="0" OR B$="." OR ASC(B$)=13)
 940        IF B THEN SOUND 2,-15,33,2
 950        IF K>1 THEN SOUND 2,-15,33,2:K=K-1:B=-1
 960     UNTIL B=0
 970
 980     A$=A$+B$
 990     IF ASC(B$)=13 THEN I=14:A$=LEFT$(A$,LEN(A$)-1):FLAG=1
1000     PRINT TAB(25+I,20);B$
1010     PRINT TAB(25+I,21);B$
1020   NEXT I
1030   IF FLAG=0 REPEAT SOUND 2,-15,33,2:B$=GET$:
                  UNTIL ASC(B$)=13
1040 ENDPROC
1050
1060
1070 DEF FNcheck(B$)
1080 IF B$="." THEN K=1
1090= VAL(B$)=0 AND NOT((B$="0") OR (B$="-")
     OR (B$="+") OR (B$="."))
1100
1110
1120 DEF PROCcalcs
1130   A=VAL(A$)
1140   total=total+A
1150   no_of_numbers=no_of_numbers+1
1160   sum_of_squares=sum_of_squares+A*A
1170   numb$=A$+","+numb$
1180 ENDPROC
1190
1200
1210 DEF PROCsetup
1220   end=0:FLAG=0:mean=0:total=0
1230   no_of_numbers=0:deviation=0
1240   sum_of_squares=0
1250   A$=""
1260 ENDPROC
```

P56   Bubble Sort

This is a demonstration to show how the classical Bubble
Sort works. The program sorts ten numbers on the screen
using MODE 7 colours and large characters.

You are asked to input the ten numbers, and the speed of
processing, the higher the number the slower the speed on
the screen.

Note that numbers displayed in yellow are being compared,
and those in red are being swapped.

COMMANDS

Key in program and type RUN.

```
100 REM Program P56 - Bubble Sort
110 DIM key%(10)
120 CLS
130 REM program sorts array of numbers into order
        on screen
140 REM The next section takes in the numbers
150 PRINT "How many digits does each no. have"
160 INPUT L
170 PRINT "Enter 10 numbers one at a time"
180 FOR I=1 TO 10
190
200    INPUT key%(I)
210    IF LEN(STR$(key%(I))) <> L THEN
          SOUND 1,-15,53,2:I=I-1
220
230 NEXT I
240 INPUT "Speed of processing (1 to 10)",SPEED
250 SPEED=SPEED*50
260 REM Print array onto screen
270 MODE 7
280 FOR I=1 TO 10
290 PRINT TAB(17,I*2);CHR$(141);key%(I);
300 PRINT TAB(17,I*2+1);CHR$(141);key%(I);
310 NEXT I
320 PROCsort(10)
330 PRINT
340 END
350
360
```

```
370 DEF PROCsort(N)
380 FOR I=1 TO (N-1)
390    FOR J=I+1 TO N
400      PROCprint(131)
410      X=INKEY(SPEED)
420      IF key%(J)>key%(I) THEN PROCswap
430      PROCprint(135)
440     NEXT J
450 NEXT I
460 ENDPROC
470
480 DEF PROCswap
490   PROCprint(129)
500   X=INKEY(SPEED)
510   temp%=key%(J)
520   key%(J)=key%(I)
530   key%(I)=temp%
540   X=INKEY(SPEED)
550   PROCprint(135)
560 ENDPROC
570
580 DEF PROCprint(X)
590   PRINT TAB(16,I*2);CHR$(141);CHR$(X);key%(I);
600   PRINT TAB(16,I*2+1);CHR$(141);CHR$(X);key%(I);
610   PRINT TAB(16,J*2);CHR$(141);CHR$(X);key%(J);
620   PRINT TAB(16,J*2+1);CHR$(141);CHR$(X);key%(J);
630 ENDPROC
```

P57 Shell Sort

This is the classical fast Shell Sort program. Similar to the bubble sort, the sorting is carried out on the screen. It can be a very useful program to try to figure out why the Shell routine works.

The sort routine itself is given in lines 310 through line 450, with a swap routine given in lines 470 through 550. These parts of the program could be used within a disc based sort program.

COMMANDS

Key in program and type RUN.
Follow instructions.
Note that SPEED=10 gives a slow sort, SPEED=1 gives a fast sort.

```
100 REM Program P57 - Shell Sort
110 MODE7
120 N=10
130 DIM array(N-1)
140 REM This program uses the Shell algorithm
        to sort an array into order on screen
150 PRINT "Enter "STR$(N)" numbers one at a time"
160 FOR I= 0 TO N-1
170   INPUT "Number",array(I)
180 NEXT I
190 INPUT "Speed of processing (1 to 10) "SPEED
200 SPEED=SPEED*100
210 CLS
220 FOR I=0 TO N-1
230   PRINT TAB(17,(I+1)*2);CHR$(141);array(I);
240   PRINT TAB(17,(I+1)*2+1);CHR$(141);array(I);
250 NEXT I
260 PROCsort(N)
270 PRINT
280 END
290
300 DEF PROCsort(N)
310 dist%=(N-1)/2
320 REPEAT
330   FOR I=dist%+1 TO N-1
340     FOR J=I-dist% TO 0 STEP -dist%
350       point=J+dist%
360       PROCprint(131)
370       Z=INKEY(SPEED)
```

```
380        IF array(J)>array(point) THEN
           PROCswap(J,point)
390          PROCprint(135)
400      NEXT J
410    NEXT I
420    dist%=dist%/2
430 UNTIL dist%=0
440 ENDPROC
450
460 DEF PROCswap(J,point)
470      PROCprint(129)
480      Z=INKEY(SPEED)
490      temp=array(J)
500      array(J)=array(point)
510      array(point)=temp
520      Z=INKEY(SPEED)
530      PROCprint(135)
540 ENDPROC
550
560 DEF PROCprint(X)
570      PRINT TAB(16,(point+1)*2);CHR$(141);CHR$(X);
            array(point);"   ";
580      PRINT TAB(16,(point+1)*2+1);CHR$(141);CHR$(X);
            array(point);"   ";
590      PRINT TAB(16,(J+1)*2);CHR$(141);CHR$(X);
            array(J);"   ";
600      PRINT TAB(16,(J+1)*2+1);CHR$(141);CHR$(X);
            array(J);"   ";
610 ENDPROC
```

P58 Merge

A common need in data processing is the ability to merge two
sorted files to produce a third sorted file.

It is quicker to sort small files and then to merge the
files to form larger ones. In this program, we mimic file
handling by using arrays. The array elements are entered via
the keyboard but the program could be amended to allow the
elements to be entered via tape files.

COMMANDS

Key in program and type RUN.
Enter array elements when prompted in increasing order.

```
100 REM Program P58 - Merge
110 MODE 7
120 PRINT "This program is used to merge two"
130 PRINT "arrays of data. Each array can hold up"
140 PRINT "to 100 data items. This program would"
150 PRINT "be used with a disc based sort routine."
160 PRINT "Each array must be entered in"
170 PRINT "increasing order."''
180 DIM array1(100),array2(100),merge(200)
190
200 I=0
210 REPEAT
220   I=I+1
230   PRINT TAB(0,10)STRING$(40," ")
240   INPUT TAB(0,10)"Array1 element (0 to finish) "
          array1(I)
250   IF array1(I)<>0 AND array1(I-1)>array1(I) THEN
      PRINT TAB(0,10)"OUT OF ORDER";STRING$(28,"."):
      I=I-1:Z=INKEY(200)
260 UNTIL array1(I)=0 OR I=100
270 n1=I-1
280
290 I=0
300 REPEAT
310   I=I+1
320   PRINT TAB(0,12)STRING$(40," ")
330   INPUT TAB(0,12)"Array2 element (0 to finish) "
          array2(I)
340   IF array2(I)<>0 AND array2(I-1)>array2(I) THEN
      PRINT TAB(0,10)"OUT OF ORDER";STRING$(28,"."):
      I=I-1:Z=INKEY(200)
350 UNTIL array2(I)=0 OR I=100
```

```
360 n2=I-1
370
380 I=1:J=1
390 REPEAT
400    IF array1(I)<array2(J) THEN merge(I+J-1)=array1(I):
       I=I+1 ELSE merge(I+J-1)=array2(J):J=J+1
410 UNTIL array1(I)=0 OR array2(J)=0
420 IF array2(J)=0 THEN PROCrunoutI
430 IF array1(I)=0 THEN PROCrunoutJ
440 CLS
450 PRINT "Array 1 consisted of :"
460 FOR I=1 TO n1
470    PRINT array1(I);
480 NEXT I
490 PRINT '"Array 2 consisted of :"
500 FOR I=1 TO n2
510    PRINT array2(I);
520 NEXT I
530 PRINT '"The merged array is :"
540 FOR I=1 TO n1+n2
550    PRINT merge(I);
560 NEXT I
570 END
580
590 DEF PROCrunoutI
600    FOR K=I TO n1
610       merge(K+J-1)=array1(K)
620    NEXT K
630 ENDPROC
640
650 DEF PROCrunoutJ
660    FOR K=J TO n2
670       merge(K+I-1)=array2(K)
680    NEXT K
690 ENDPROC
```

P59 Binary Search

If you have a mass of data sorted into order, then it is
very inefficient to search for a particular item in a
sequential manner. For instance, when looking for a word in
a dictionary you would not consider every word in sequence
until you found the required entry.

A more efficient search method is to open the dictionary in
the middle and decide which half of the book holds your
word. You then take this half of the book and half it again.
This routine is repeated until the page holding your word is
found.

This program performs a similar search on a set of data - a
price list. It could of course be used in any searching
problem.

COMMANDS

Key in program and type RUN.
Enter item required from price list.


```
100 REM Program P59 - Binary Search
110 DIM item$(100),price(100)
120 MODE 7
130 PRINT TAB(7,12)"B I N A R Y   S E A R C H"
140 Z=INKEY(300)
150 CLS
160 PRINT "This program shows how the computer"
170 PRINT "can be used to quickly look up a set of"
180 PRINT "data. We assume that the data have been"
190 PRINT "sorted into alphabetic order, for the"
200 PRINT "purposes of this program, the data are"
210 PRINT "held in data statements. In this case"
220 PRINT "the data constitute a price list."
230 PRINT '"Press any key to continue"
240 Z=GET
250 CLS
260 I=0
270 REPEAT
280   I=I+1
290   READ item$(I),price(I)
300 UNTIL item$(I)="ZZZ"
310 N%=I-1
320
```

```
330 REPEAT
340    INPUT ''"Which item do you require? "item$
350
360    M%=N%/2
370    L%=M%
380    found=FALSE
390    not_there=FALSE
400    REPEAT
410      IF item$<item$(M%+1) AND item$>item$(M%-1) AND NOT found
         THEN not_there=TRUE
420      IF item$=item$(M%) THEN found=TRUE
430      IF item$<item$(M%) THEN L%=L%/2:M%=M%-L%+(L%=0)
440      IF item$>item$(M%) THEN L%=L%/2:M%=M%+L%-(L%=0)
450      REPEAT
460          IF M%>N% THEN L%=L%/2:M%=M%-L%+(L%=0)
470      UNTIL NOT(M%>N%)
480    UNTIL found OR not_there
490
500    IF found THEN PRINT '''item$(M%),price(M%)
         ELSE PRINT ''"Item not in list"
510    INPUT '''"Another",res$
520 UNTIL LEFT$(res$,1)<>"Y"
530 END
540
550 DATA APPLES,30.1,BAG,12.09,BAG-BLUE,56.34,BANANA,3.10,
        BANGER,123.23,BEER-EXPORT,0.45,BEER-LAGER,0.55
555 DATA BEER-STOUT,0.67,BOOZE,4.34,BOTTLE,90.2,
        BOTTLE-GREEN,3.45,BOVRIL,0.75
560 DATA CABBAGE,0.76,CANADA DRY,0.78,CANADIAN CLUB,7.35,
        CARROTS,0.30,COD LIVER OIL,0.76,COMPUTERS,299.99
565 DATA COOKERS,0.65,CRAB-APPLES,0.00
570 DATA DIGGERS,4567.34,DISC DRIVES,250.67,DISCS DDDS,2.55,
        DISCS SSSS,1.80,DOZERS,123456.67
580 DATA EMPIRE BISCUITS,.70,EMULATOR,5677,ENAMEL-RED,7.35,
        ENAMEL-WHITE,8.35,ENGINE-CAR,50.56,
        ENGINE-SCOOTER,45.76,ET CETERA,0,EWE,36.25,
        EXPLOSIVE,105.67,FABRIC-BLACK,12.45
590 DATA FABRIC-BLUE,9.67,FABRIC-RED,11.6,FABRIC-WHITE,56.0,
        FAN,5.79,FARE,0.98,FARM,1000000,FEATHER PILLOW,78.67
600 DATA ZZZ,0
```

P60 Permutations

This program can be used to find the number of permutations of n objects taken r at a time. This is a very useful routine in statistics.

COMMANDS

Key in program and type RUN.
Follow instructions.

```
100 REM Program P60 - Permutations
110 MODE 7
120 PRINT "This program can be used to find the"
130 PRINT "number of permutations of n objects"
140 PRINT "taken r at a time."
150 PRINT '"For example, suppose there are 4 people"
160 PRINT "in a race, then how many ways can the"
170 PRINT "first three positions be filled?"
180 PRINT ''"Suppose the racers are called A,B,C & D"
190 PRINT "then possible finishing positions "
200 PRINT "would be:"
210 PRINT '"ABC BAC BCA CAB CBA ACB"
220 PRINT "ABD ADB BDA BAD DBA DAB"
230 PRINT "ACD ADC CAD CDA DAC DCA"
240 PRINT "BCD BDC CBD CDB DCB DBC"
250 PRINT '"In this example there are 24 ways of"
260 PRINT "placing the first 3 in the race"
270 PRINT ''"PRESS ANY KEY TO CONTINUE"
280 X=GET
290 CLS
300 PRINT "This program will allow the user to"
310 PRINT "calculate the number of permutations"
320 INPUT '''"Number of objects "n
330 INPUT "Value of r - the size of the group "r
340 perms=FNfact(n)/FNfact(n-r)
350 PRINT ''''"Number of permutations="STR$(perms)
360 END
370
380 DEF FNfact(r)
390 IF r>33 THEN PRINT "TOO BIG":=0
400 IF r=1 THEN =1 ELSE =r*FNfact(r-1)
```

128

P61 Combinations

This progam finds the number of combinations of n objects
taken r at a time.

COMMANDS

Key in program and type RUN.
Follow instructions.

```
100 REM Program P61 - Combinations
110 MODE 7
120 PRINT "This program can be used to find the"
130 PRINT "number of combinations of n objects"
140 PRINT "taken r at a time."
150 PRINT '"For example, suppose we wish to make up"
160 PRINT "a committee of 3 people out of a"
170 PRINT "pool of 4 people. How many ways can"
180 PRINT "this be done?"
190 PRINT '"Suppose the people are called A,B,C and"
200 PRINT "D, then possible combinations would be"
210 PRINT '"ABC ABD ACD BCD"
220 PRINT'"In this example there are 4 ways of"
230 PRINT "making up the committee"
240 PRINT '"PRESS ANY KEY TO CONTINUE"
250 X=GET
260 CLS
270 PRINT "This program will allow the user to"
280 PRINT "calculate the number of combinations"
290 INPUT '''"How many objects are to be selected from "n
300 INPUT "Value of r - the size of the group "r
310 combs=FNfact(n)/FNfact(n-r)/FNfact(r)
320 PRINT ''''"Number of combinations="STR$(combs)
330 END
340
350 DEF FNfact(r)
360 IF r>33 THEN PRINT "TOO BIG":=0
370 IF r=1 THEN =1 ELSE =r*FNfact(r-1)
```

P62 Least Squares

This program uses the method of least squares to find the best straight line through a set of data points.

The straight line found is in the form

    Y=MX+B

with the parameters M and B found in lines 280 and 290. When the equation is found, it is plotted on the screen along with the data points.

COMMANDS

Key in program and type RUN.
Enter the data items in the form X,Y.

```
100 REM Program P62 - Least Squares
110 @%=&20205
120 MODE 7
130 PRINT "LEAST SQUARES"
140 INPUT ''"How many data points?",N
150 PRINT ''
160 DIM X(N),Y(N)
170 FOR I=1 TO N
180    INPUT "X=",X(I),"Y=",Y(I)
190    sum_x=sum_x + X(I)
200    sum_x_sq=sum_x_sq + X(I)*X(I)
210    sum_y=sum_y + Y(I)
220    sum_xy=sum_xy + X(I)*Y(I)
230 NEXT I
240
250 D=N*sum_x_sq - sum_x*sum_x
260 IF D=0 THEN PRINT "NO FIT POSSIBLE!!!":END
270
280 M=(N*sum_xy - sum_x*sum_y)/D
290 B=sum_y/N - M*sum_x/N
300 REM plotting routine
310 max_x=X(1):min_x=X(1)
320 max_y=Y(1):min_y=Y(1)
330 FOR I=2 TO N
340    IF max_x<X(I) THEN max_x=X(I)
350    IF min_x>X(I) THEN min_x=X(I)
360    IF max_y<Y(I) THEN max_y=Y(I)
370    IF min_y>Y(I) THEN min_y=Y(I)
380 NEXT I
```

```
390 MODE 4
400 IF min_x>0 THEN min_x=0
410 IF min_y>0 THEN min_y=0
420 range_x=max_x - min_x
430 range_y=max_y - min_y
440 REM plot will not work for all negative data
450 scale_x=1200/range_x
460 scale_y=1000/range_y
470 VDU 29,ABS(min_x*scale_x);ABS(min_y*scale_y);
480 MOVE min_x*scale_x,0:DRAW max_x*scale_x,0
490 MOVE 0,min_y*scale_y:DRAW 0,max_y*scale_y
500 VDU5
510 FOR I=1 TO N
520   MOVE X(I)*scale_x,Y(I)*scale_y
530   PRINT CHR$(8);"+";
540 NEXT I
550 MOVE min_x*scale_x,(M*min_x + B)*scale_y
560 DRAW max_x*scale_x,(M*max_x + B)*scale_y
570 PRINT TAB(0,0)"Line is Y="M"*X+"B
580 END
```

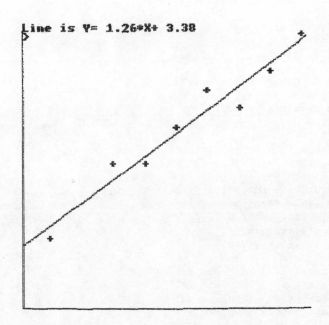

P63 Number of Days

It can be interesting in many everyday problems to calculate
the number of days between two dates. This program does this
by calculating the number of days from day 0 of the
Gregorian Calendar for each date and then calculating the
number of days between the two dates.

COMMANDS

Key in program and type RUN.
Enter Gregorian dates when prompted.

```
100 REM Program P63 - Number of Days
110 CLS
120 PRINT "Enter first date of interest"
130 INPUT "Day (1-31) " day_1
140 INPUT "Month (1-12) " month_1
150 INPUT "Year (eg 1982) " year_1
160 PRINT '''"Enter second date of interest"
170 INPUT "Day (1-31) " day_2
180 INPUT "Month (1-12) " month_2
190 INPUT "Year (eg 1982) " year_2
200 no_of_days=FN_days(day_2,month_2,year_2) -
            FN_days(day_1,month_1,year_1)
210 PRINT '''"The number of days between the two "
220 PRINT "dates is "no_of_days
230 END
240 DEF FN_days(d,m,y)
250 RESTORE
260 FOR I=1 TO m
270   READ days_this_year
280 NEXT I
290 DATA 0,31,59,90,120,151,181,212,243,273,304,334
300 days_this_year=days_this_year+d
310 days_since_0=days_this_year +y*365 + INT(y/4) +1
            - INT(y/100) + INT(y/400)
320  IF (y MOD 4=0) AND (m<3)  THEN
        days_since_0=days_since_0 - 1
330 =days_since_0
```

P64 Digital Clock

This program exhibits a digital clock on the screen.

COMMANDS

Key in program and type RUN.
Enter time when requested.

```
100 REM Program P64 - Digital Clock
110 MODE 7
120 @%=2
130 INPUT "Hour "hour
140 INPUT "Minute " min
150 INPUT "Second " sec
160 CLS
170 VDU 23;8202;0;0;0;
180 TIME=0
190 PRINT TAB(0,12)CHR$(141);
200 PRINT TAB(0,13)CHR$(141);
210 PRINT TAB(16,12)":"
220 PRINT TAB(16,13)":"
230 PRINT TAB(19,12)":"
240 PRINT TAB(19,13)":"
250 REPEAT
260    TIME=0
270    hour=hour MOD 24
280    REPEAT
290      IF hour>0 THEN TIME=0
300      PRINT TAB(14,12) hour
310      PRINT TAB(14,13) hour
320      hour=hour+1
330      min=min MOD 60
340      REPEAT
350        IF min>0 THEN TIME=0
360        PRINT TAB(17,12) min
370        PRINT TAB(17,13) min
380        min=min+1
390        sec=sec MOD 60
400        REPEAT
410          IF sec>0 THEN TIME=0
420          PRINT TAB(20,12) sec
430          PRINT TAB(20,13) sec
440          sec=sec+1
450          REPEAT UNTIL TIME=100
460        UNTIL sec=60
470      UNTIL min=60
480    UNTIL hour=24
490 UNTIL 0
```

P65 Kitchen Timer

A useful program for the kitchen here, the program displays
the time that has yet to elapse before your meal is ready.
When time reaches zero, an alarm sounds.

COMMANDS

Key in program and type RUN.
Enter setting when requested.

```
100 REM Program P65 - Kitchen Timer
110 MODE7
120 @%=3
130 PRINT TAB(12,12)"K I T C H E N"
140 PRINT TAB(12,14)" T I M E R"
150 Z=INKEY(300)
160 CLS
170 FOR I=0 TO 24
180    PRINT CHR$(131);CHR$(157);CHR$(133)
190 NEXT I
200 PRINT TAB(5,5)"What setting do you require?";
210 INPUT TAB(5,6)"Hours="hours
220 INPUT TAB(5,7)"Minutes="mins
230 INPUT TAB(5,8)"Seconds=" secs
240 IF secs>0 THEN secs=secs-1
250 PRINT TAB(5,5) STRING$(30," ");
260 PRINT TAB(5,6) STRING$(20," ");
270 PRINT TAB(5,7) STRING$(20," ");
280 PRINT TAB(5,8) STRING$(20," ");
290
300 PRINT TAB(4,12)CHR$(141)
310 PRINT TAB(4,13)CHR$(141)
320 REPEAT
330   REPEAT
340     REPEAT
350       TIME=0
360       REPEAT UNTIL TIME=100
370       PRINT TAB(15,12) hours,mins,secs
380       PRINT TAB(15,13) hours,mins,secs
390       secs=secs-1
400     UNTIL secs=-1
410     mins=mins-1
420     secs=59
430   UNTIL mins=-1
440   hours=hours-1
450   mins=59
460 UNTIL hours=-1
470
480 SOUND 1,-15,53,-1
```

P66   Recipes

In this program, I have recorded some of my favourite
recipes. These are based on recipes in "Favourite Family
Cookbook" by Norma MacMillan, Octopus (1978).

Notice the use of the RESTORE statements in lines 210 and
300. This is an example of direct accessing of data. We do
not read through the whole of the recipe list to find the
one required, but restore the DATA pointer to the correct
line. You can use this basic structure to build up your own
recipes.

Although I have included my own recipes, it would perhaps be
better if you replaced my data statements with your own.

COMMANDS

Key in program and type RUN.
Follow the menus as presented.

```
100 REM Program P66 - Recipes
110 CLS
120 PRINT '''"     R E C I P E   M E N U"
130 PRINT '''
140 PRINT "       1. Hors d'Oeuvres"
150 PRINT "       2. Soups"
160 PRINT "       3. Fish"
170 PRINT "       4. Meat"
180
190 PROCrubric
200 section=choice%*1000
210 RESTORE section
220 READ menu_title$
230 CLS
240 PRINT '''"       "menu_title$'''
250 FOR I=1 TO 4
260   READ recipe_name$
270   PRINT I". "recipe_name$
280 NEXT I
290 PROCrubric
300 RESTORE section+choice%*10
310 CLS
```

```
320 READ recipe_name$
330 PRINT CHR$(141);recipe_name$
340 PRINT CHR$(141);recipe_name$
350 PRINT ''
360 ingredient$=""
370 REPEAT
380   PRINT ingredient$
390   READ ingredient$
400 UNTIL ingredient$="end"
410 INPUT '"Another",ans$
420 IF LEFT$(ans$,1)="Y" THEN RUN ELSE END
430
440 DEF PROCrubric
450 PRINT '''"Enter the appropriate number for the"
460 PRINT "recipe of your choice";
470 INPUT "  "choice%
480 ENDPROC
490
500


1000 DATA H o r s   d' O e u v r e s,Kipper pate,Egg Mayonn
aise,Mushrooms a la grecque,Grilled Grapefruit
1010 DATA K i p p e r   p a t e,2 tblesp unsalted butter,1/
2lb kipper fillets,1 cup cream cheese,1/2 garlic clove-crush
ed,juice of 1/2 lemon,black pepper,,,
1011 DATA Melt butter in frying pan,add kippers,cook till s
oft,remove and cool then flake fish
1012 DATA Blend fish cheese etc till smooth,Serve chilled w
ith pepper,end
1020 DATA E g g  M a y o n n a i s e,4 large lettuce leaves
,8 sprigs watercress,4 eggs - hard boiled and halved,1 1/4 c
ups mayonnaise,pinch of paprika,,,
1021 DATA Put a lettuce leaf on each of 4 plates.,Add 2 spr
igs of watercress to each,Place eggs in centre flat side dow
n.,Pour over mayonnaise and add paprika,end,
1030 DATA Mushrooms a la grecque,1 1/4 cups water,small oni
on - chopped,2 tblesp olive oil,1 teasp tomato paste,salt n
pepper,bouquet garni and lemon juice
1031 DATA 3 cups small button mushrooms,parsley to garnish
1032 DATA Put all except mushrooms and garnish,into saucepa
n and simmer for 5 minutes.,Add mushrooms and simmer for 10
minutes.,Remove mushrooms.
1033 DATA Boil liquid until 3-4 tblesp left.,Pour over mush
rooms and serve with,parsley,end,
1040 DATA G r i l l e d   G r a p e f r u i t,2 large grape
fruits - halved,4 teasp medium sherry,4 tblesp brown sugar,1
tblesp butter - cut into 4 pieces,,,
```

1041 DATA Loosen segments of grapefruit and,remove seeds. D
rain halves onto kitchen,paper for a few minutes.,Place grap
efruit halves in grill pan,cut sides up. Sprinkle each with
sugar,and sherry.
1042 DATA Top each with butter - grill until,bubbling,end,

2000 DATA S o u p s,Borsch,Pea Soup,Oxtail Soup,French Onio
n Soup
2010 DATA B o r s c h,2 tblesp butter,large onion - peeled
and sliced,large carrot - peeled and grated,2 large cooked b
eetroots - sliced
2011 DATA 1/2 small head red cabbage - shredded,1 tblsp tom
ato paste,1 tblsp vinegar & 1 tblsp sugar,salt n pepper,5 cu
ps beef stock,1 1/4 cups sour cream to serve,,
2012 DATA Melt butter in pan and cook vegetables,gently for
5 minutes. Stir in other,ingredients and simmer for 20-30 m
ins,until veg are tender. Serve with cream,end,
2020 DATA P e a   S o u p,2 tblesp butter & 1 tblesp olive
oil,1 onion & 2 celery stalks - chopped
2021 DATA 2 cups shelled peas,1 small ham bone,2 cups chick
en stock,1 tblsp cornflour,1 1/4 cups milk,salt n pepper,,
2022 DATA Melt butter and oil in pan - fry celery,and onion
. Cook peas for 5 mins. Add,bone & stock then boil for 40 mi
ns.,Remove bone and puree soup.,Dissolve flour in milk and a
dd to soup.,Simmer until thick. Serve hot.,end,
2030 DATA O x t a i l   S o u p,4 tblspns oil & 4 1/2 pts w
ater,1 oxtail - cut into pieces,2 onions 2 carrots 2 celery
- chopped
2031 DATA1 turnip chopped,salt n pepper,1 14 oz can of tom
atoes,2 tblsp flour & 4 tblsp sherry,,
2032 DATA Brown oxtail and fry veg till soft. Add,to water
with salt n pepper. Simmer for,4 hours. Remove oxtails and c
ut meat,from bones. Remove fat from soup and,return meat. Th
icken with sherry and,flour. Serve hot.,end,
2040 DATA F r e n c h   O n i o n   S o u p,2 tblspn butter
& 2 tblspn olive oil,1 garlic clove - crushed,3 large slice
d onions,5 cups beef stock
2041 DATA salt n pepper,8-12 slices French bread,3/4 cup ch
eese,,
2042 DATA Fry garlic and onions for 20 mins,do not brown to
o much. Simmer with salt n pepper for 30 mins.,Toast bread.,
Serve soup hot with toast and cheese,end,

3000 DATA F i s h,Trout with Almonds,Salmon Steaks,Finnan H
addie,Scallops and Bacon
3010 DATA T r o u t   w i t h   A l m o n d s,1/4 cup plain
flour,salt n pepper,4 large trout - cleaned,1/3 cup butter,
1/2 cup almond flakes,2 teaspn lemon juice,lemon and parsley
to garnish,,

3011 DATA Mix flour with salt n pepper and coat,the trout.
Melt butter in pan and brown,trout quickly on both sides. Co
ok trout,until tender. Remove fish and keep hot.
3012 DATA Cook almonds in pan until golden.,Stir in lemon j
uice. Pour liquid and,almonds over fish and garnish.,end,
3020 DATA S a l m o n   S t e a k s,4 salmon steaks,1/4 cup
butter cut into 4,4 of - 1/2 bay leaf:onion slices,4 of - s
liver lemon rind:thyme sprig,4 of - parsley sprig: salt n pe
pper,
3021 DATA Divide ingredients into individual,portions. Wrap
each in foil and bake in,a moderate oven (180 C:350 F:Gas M
ark 4,for 15-20 mins. Serve steaks hot without herbs.,end,
3030 DATA F i n n a n   H a d d i e,1 1/2 lb smoked haddock
- chopped,1 1/4 cups milk,2/3 cup single cream,2 tblsp butt
er,pepper,6 eggs,,
3031 DATA Place fish in baking dish. Put milk,and cream and
butter in pan and heat,until butter is melted. Pour over fi
sh.,Bake in moderate oven(180 C:350 F:Gas,Mark 4) for 20 min
s.
3032 DATA Poach eggs 5 mins before fish is ready.,Top fish
mixture with eggs and serve.,end,
3040 DATA S c a l l o p s   a n d   B a c o n,16-20 shelled
scallops,salt n pepper and lemon juice,16-20 bacon slices,,
3041 DATA Sprinkle scallops with salt n pepper,and lemon ju
ice. Stretch bacon rashers,with flat knife. Wrap rasher roun
d each,scallop and secure with cocktail stick.,Grill slowly
till cooked - 5 mins and,serve with tartare sauce.,end,

4000 DATA M e a t,Neapolitan Steak,Wiener Schnitzel,Lamb Cu
rry,Pork 'n Orange
4010 DATA N e a p o l i t a n   S t e a k,4 sirloin steaks,
3 cups peeled n chopped tomatoes,2 tblsp olive oil,2 chopped
garlic cloves,1 tblsp chopped parsley,1/2 teasp dried oregan
o :1 teasp sugar,salt n pepper,,
4011 DATA Boil toms oil garlic parsley sugar,salt n pepper
and simmer for 5 mins.,Grill steaks and pour sauce over.,Ser
ve hot.,end,
4020 DATA W i e n e r   S c h n i t z e l,4 veal escalopes
pounded thin,juice of 2 lemons,salt n pepper and large beate
n egg,1 cup dry breadcrumbs,3 tblsp butter,lemon wedges to g
arnish,,
4021 DATA Marinate veal in lemon with salt n,pepper for 1 h
our. Dip veal in egg and,coat with breadcrumbs. Fry veal in,
butter till golden brown.,end,
4030 DATA L a m b   C u r r y,2lb lean lamb cubed,2/3 cup y
oghurt :2 teasp garam masala,1 tblsp curry powder,2 tblsp bu
tter :2 tblsp oil,2 chopped onions : crushed garlic clove,sa
lt n pepper n lemon juice
4031 DATA 2/3 cup dried fruit : 2 tblsp almonds,,

4032 DATA Mix yoghurt with garam masala and curry,Add lamb
cubes and marinate for 4 hours,Fry onions and garlic till so
ft. Stir,in lamb + yoghurt & salt n pepper and,lemon juice.
Cook for 5 mins then add
    4033 DATA fruit and almonds. Simmer till tender,end,
    4040 DATA P o r k   'n   O r a n g e,1/4 cup plain flour :
salt n pepper,1 1/2lb pork fillet cut into cubes,2 tblsp but
ter : small onion chopped,1 chopped green pepper no pith or
seeds,grated rind and juice of 2 oranges
    4041 DATA 1 tblespn Worcestershire sauce,2/3 cup beef stock
,1 peeled segmented orange,,
    4042 DATA Mix flour salt n pepper in bag. Add,pork cubes an
d shake to coat. Fry onion,and pepper in butter till soft. B
rown,pork. Stir in orange rind and juice,add stock and sauce
. Simmer for 10 mins,add orange segs and cook for 2 mins
    4043 DATA Serve hot.,end,
    5000 REM End of program data.

Pork 'n Orange

1/4 cup plain flour : salt n pepper
1 1/2lb pork fillet cut into cubes
2 tblespns butter : small onion chopped
1 chopped green pepper no pith or seeds
grated rind and juice of 2 oranges
1 tblespn Worcestershire sauce
2/3 cup beef stock
1 peeled segmented orange

Mix flour salt n pepper in bag. Add
pork cubes and shake to coat. Fry onion
and pepper in butter till soft. Brown
pork. Stir in orange rind and juice
add stock and sauce. Simmer for 10 mins
add orange segs and cook for 2 mins
serve hot

Another?_

P67   Encoder

This program can be used to code a secret message. The system used for the encoding is very simple. You are asked for a key word, the characters of which are used to offset the characters of the secret message. The program uses all the printable characters of the BBC, so that characters such as space, full stop and comma, etc are also encoded. The encoding routine is held in lines 420 to 460.

EXAMPLE

MESSAGE	ABCD
KEY WORD	12
SECRET CODE IS	RTTV

Note the use of VDU21 and VDU6 to switch screen on and off.

COMMANDS

Key in program and type RUN.
Type secret message finish with RETURN. (Note that it will not appear on the screen.)
Type in secret key word, finish with RETURN. (Note that it will not appear on the screen.)

You have six seconds to take down the message.

```
100 REM Program P67 - Encoder
110 DIM offset(25),characters(255),codes(255)
120 MODE4
130 PRINT '''"This program can be used to produce a"
140 PRINT "coded version of a secret message."
150 PRINT "The program bases the encoding on a key"
160 PRINT "word which you specify."
170 PRINT '"Neither the key word nor the message is"
180 PRINT "seen on the screen."
190 PRINT '"What is your message?"
200 VDU 21
210 INPUT LINE message$
220 VDU 6
230 PRINT "What is the key word?"
```

```
240 VDU 21
250 INPUT key_word$
260 VDU 6
270
280
290 FOR I=1 TO LEN(key_word$)
300    offset(I)=ASC(MID$(key_word$,I,1))-32
310 NEXT I
320
330 FOR I=1 TO LEN(message$)
340    characters(I)=ASC(MID$(message$,I,1))-32
350 NEXT I
360
370 REM encode
380 code$=""
390 J=0
400
410
420 FOR I=1 TO LEN(message$)
430    codes(I)=(characters(I)+offset(J+1)) MOD 93
440    code$=code$+CHR$(codes(I)+32)
450    J=(J+1) MOD LEN(key_word$)
460 NEXT I
470
480
490 PRINT "Your coded message is"
500 PRINT code$
510 PRINT ''"Press any key to finish"
520 A$=INKEY$(600)
530 CLS
540 END
```

P68   Decoder

This program decodes secret messages created by program P66.
You need to have the secret message plus the key word to
find the original message.

EXAMPLE

Coded message	RTIV
Key word	12
Message	ABCD

COMMANDS

Key in program and type RUN.
Type in coded message.
Type in key word.
You have six seconds to take down message.

```
100 REM Program P68 - Decoder
110 DIM offset(25),characters(255),codes(255)
120 MODE4
130 PRINT '''"This program can be used to produce a"
140 PRINT "decoded version of a secret message."
150 PRINT "The program bases the decoding on a key"
160 PRINT "word which you specify."
170 PRINT '"Neither the key word nor the message is"
180 PRINT "seen on the screen"
190 PRINT '"What is your coded message?"
200 VDU 21
210 INPUT LINE code$
220 VDU 6
230 PRINT "What is the key word?"
240 VDU 21
250 INPUT key_word$
260 VDU 6
270
280
290 FOR I=1 TO LEN(key_word$)
300     offset(I)=ASC(MID$(key_word$,I,1))-32
310 NEXT I
320
```

```
330 FOR I=1 TO LEN(code$)
340    characters(I)=ASC(MID$(code$,I,1))-32
350 NEXT I
360
370 REM decode
380 message$=""
390 J=0
400
410
420 FOR I=1 TO LEN(code$)
430    codes(I)=(characters(I)-offset(J+1)) MOD 93
440    IF codes(I)<0 THEN codes(I)=93+codes(I)
450    message$=message$+CHR$(codes(I)+32)
460    J=(J+1) MOD LEN(key_word$)
470 NEXT I
480
490
500 PRINT "Your decoded message is"
510 PRINT message$
520 PRINT ''"Press any key to finish"
530 A$=INKEY$(600)
540 CLS
550 END
```

P69 The Game Of Life   MODEL B ONLY

This program is a variation of the game of LIFE developed by
John Conway, but I have not used the classical rules for life
for the purposes of this program.

The program mimics the evolution of a colony of bugs.
I decided to use the following rules for determining whether
a bug will live from one period to another, or whether it is
to die or whether a baby bug is to be procreated.

The screen shows a picture of a generation of the bug colony.
The program then has two passes over the screen.

Pass one determines whether a bug has to die or not, or
whether a new bug has to be procreated. A bug dies from
overcrowding if it has more than three neighbours, or from
loneliness if it has less than two neighbours, then a baby
bug is generated.

Pass two removes all dead bugs from the screen and shows baby
bugs attaining adulthood.

To start off the program, the initial state of the colony is
described by giving the position of the bugs.

COMMAND

Key in program and type RUN.
Follow instructions.

```
100 REM Program P69 - The Game of Life
110 DIM X(100),Y(100)
120 VDU 23,224,60,126,153,255,126,90,90,153
130 bug$=CHR$(224)
140 VDU 23,225,0,60,126,201,255,102,60,0
150 babybug$=CHR$(225)
160 VDU 23,226,153,90,90,126,254,126,56,0
170 deadbug$=CHR$(226)
180
190 CLS
200 PRINT TAB(12,12) "L I F E"
210 X=INKEY(300):CLS
```

```
220 REM Set up initial state
230 I=0
240 PRINT "Enter co-ords of bugs,(99,99 to end)"
250 REPEAT
260 I=I+1
270    INPUT X(I),Y(I)
280 UNTIL X(I)=99
290 MODE5
300 COLOUR 1
310 FOR J=1 TO I-1
320   PRINT TAB(X(J),Y(J)) bug$;
330 NEXT J
340
350
360
370 FOR I%=0 TO 24
380 REPEAT
390    FOR X%=0 TO 19
400    FOR Y%=0 TO 31
410       K%=FNchar(X%,Y%)
420       IF K%=224 OR K%=225 OR K%=128 OR K%=129 THEN
             PROCpoint_flag(X%,Y%)
430    NEXT Y%
440    NEXT X%
450 REM Pass two
460    FOR X%=0 TO 19
470      FOR Y%=0 TO 31
480         PROCchangestate(X%,Y%)
490       NEXT Y%
500    NEXT X%
510 UNTIL 0
520
530 DEF PROCpoint_flag(X,Y)
540   LOCAL K%,neighbours%
550   FOR I=-1 TO 1
560     FOR J=-1 TO 1
570       K%=FNchar(X+I,Y+J)
580       IF K%=224 OR K%=225 OR K%=128 OR K%=129 THEN
            neighbours%=neighbours%+1
590     NEXT J
600   NEXT I
610 COLOUR 2
620   IF neighbours%>3 OR neighbours%<2 THEN
          PRINT TAB(X,Y) deadbug$
630   IF neighbours%=2 THEN PROCbaby(X,Y)
640 ENDPROC
650
```

```
660 DEF PROCbaby(X,Y)
670    FOR I=-1 TO 1
680      FOR J=-1 TO 1
690        COLOUR 3
700        IF FNchar(X+I,Y+J)=32 THEN
             PRINT TAB(X+I,Y+J) babybug$:I=1:J=1
710      NEXT J
720     NEXT I
730 ENDPROC
740
750 DEF PROCchangestate(X,Y)
760    COLOUR 0
770    L%=FNchar(X,Y)
780    IF L%=226 OR L%=130 THEN PRINT TAB(X,Y) " "
790    COLOUR 1
800    IF L%=225 OR L%=129 THEN PRINT TAB(X,Y) bug$
810 ENDPROC
820
830
840 DEF FNchar(u,v)
850 VDU31,u,v
860 A%=135
870 =(USR(&FFF4) AND &FF00)/&100
```

P70 Biorhythms

It has been said that a human being has predictable ups and downs. The proponents of biorhythms state that there are three main cycles in life - the Physical,Emotional and Intellectual.

This program is used to show the biorhythms for any particular person at any point in his life. The program displays the three biorhythms for a period of twenty days starting from the date of interest.

The program can be used to display the biorhythms for any person in history. Note that dates must be in the Gregorian calendar.

COMMANDS

Key in program and type RUN.
Follow instructions.
Interpret biorhythm.

```
100 REM Program P70 - Biorhythms
110 MODE 7
120 @%=9
130 PRINT TAB(12,12) "BIORHYTHMS"
140 X=INKEY(200)
150 CLS
160 PRINT "Enter date of interest"
170 INPUT "Day (1-31) " day
180 INPUT "Month (1-12) " month
190 INPUT "Year (eg 1982) " year
200 PRINT '''"Enter date of birth of subject"
210 INPUT "Day (1-31) " b_day
220 INPUT "Month (1-12) " b_month
230 INPUT "Year (eg 1982) " b_year
240 days_alive=FN_days(day,month,year) -
                FN_days(b_day,b_month,b_year)
250 PRINT '"The subject has lived for "days_alive" days"
260 PRINT '''"Press key to continue":x=GET
270 MODE 5
280 VDU 19,0,5;0;
290 MOVE 0,512
300 GCOL 0,2
310 DRAW 1279,512
320 FOR X=0 TO 1280 STEP 64
330     MOVE X,500
340     DRAW X,524
350 NEXT X
```

```
360 COLOUR 1
370 PRINT TAB(0,1)"Physical ";
380 PROCplot(23,1)
390 COLOUR 2
400 PRINT "Emotional    ";
410 PROCplot(28,2)
420 COLOUR 3
430 PRINT "Intellectual"
440 VDU 5
450 PROCplot(33,3)
460 END
470 DEF PROCplot(p,c)
480 MOVE 0,512
490 GCOL 0,c
500  FOR X=0 TO 1279 STEP 8
510    Y=INT(400*SIN(2*PI*(days_alive + X/64)/p)+512)
520    PLOT 5,X,Y
530  NEXT X
540 ENDPROC
550 DEF FN_days(d,m,y)
560 RESTORE
570 FOR I=1 TO m
580   READ days_this_year
590 NEXT I
600 DATA 0,31,59,90,120,151,181,212,243,273,304,334
610 days_this_year=days_this_year+d
620 days_since_0=days_this_year +y*365 + INT(y/4) +1
                - INT(y/100) + INT(y/400)
630  IF (y MOD 4=0) AND (m<3)
     THEN days_since_0=days_since_0 - 1
640 =days_since_0
```

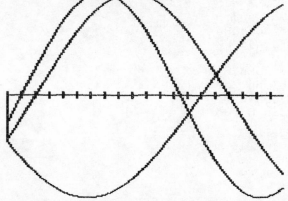

148

P71 Anagrams

A nice short program here which finds all cyclic
permutations of a word entered. So this is not actually a
full anagram program.

COMMANDS

Key in program and type RUN.
Enter word.


```
100 REM Program P71 - Anagrams
110 MODE 7
120 PRINT "This program prints arrangements of"
130 PRINT "the letters of a word which you input."
140 PRINT "Only cyclic permutations of the letters"
150 PRINT "of the word are considered."
160 INPUT ''"Word is "word$
170 FOR I=1 TO LEN(word$)
180   PRINT MID$(word$,I)+LEFT$(word$,I-1)
190 NEXT I
200 END
```

```
This program prints arrangements of
the letters of a word which you input.
Only cyclic permutations of the letters
of the word are considered.
Word is John Gordon
John Gordon
ohn GordonJ
hn GordonJo
n GordonJoh
 GordonJohn
GordonJohn
ordonJohn G
rdonJohn Go
donJohn Gor
onJohn Gord
nJohn Gordo
```

P72 Magic Matrix

This program is based on an interesting idea presented in Martin Gardener's book "Mathematical Puzzles and Diversions" (Bell 1964).

The program generates a matrix which is not a magic square, but which has some interesting properties.

I have found that this is an amusing party trick, even if I simply draw the matrix out on a piece of paper. The basic idea is rather simple, see if you can work it out.

COMMANDS

Key in program and type RUN.
Follow instructions.

```
100 REM Program P72 - Magic Matrix
110 MODE 7
120 PRINT "This program produces a square array "
130 PRINT "with the following interesting property."
140 PRINT "You are asked to pick any number in "
150 PRINT "the square. You indicate this by row"
160 PRINT "and column number. The computer will "
170 PRINT "then block out all other numbers in"
180 PRINT "that row and column. This continues"
190 PRINT "until only one number remains."
200 PRINT ''"Notice that the sum of the numbers"
210 PRINT "remaining is the same as that at the"
220 PRINT "bottom of the screen."
230 PRINT "Press any key to continue"
240 Z=GET
250 CLS
260 DIM X(5,2)
270 FOR I=1 TO 5
280    X(I,1)=RND(30)
290    X(I,2)=RND(30)
300    SUM=SUM+X(I,2)+X(I,1)
310 NEXT I
320 DIM A(5,5), ROW(5), COLUMN(5)
330 @%=3
340 PRINT ''''
```

```
350 FOR I=1 TO 5
360   FOR J=1 TO 5
370     A(I,J)=X(I,2)+X(J,1)
380     PRINT A(I,J);
390   NEXT J
400   PRINT
410 NEXT I
420
430 s$=""
440 FOR J=1 TO 5
450 PRINT TAB(0,20)"SUM ="SUM
460 INPUT TAB(0,15)"ROW=",R
470 INPUT TAB(0,16)"COLUMN=",C
480 IF ROW(R)>0 OR COLUMN(C)>0 THEN 460
490 ROW(R)=1: COLUMN(C)=1
500 FOR I=0 TO 4
510   PRINT TAB(I*3,4+R)" . "
520   PRINT TAB(3*(C-1),5+I)" . "
530 NEXT I
540 PRINT TAB(20,4+R) A(R,C)
550 s$=s$+"+"+STR$(A(R,C))
560 NEXT J
570 PRINT TAB(4,21)"="MID$(s$,2)
```

P73 Dice

A gambler's delight, this program rolls three dice. At the moment the dice are fair, but it is possible to seed the random number generator to make sure that the sequence of random numbers is predictable.

To do this enter the following line,

    115 X=RND(-5)

then experiment with the results.

COMMANDS

Key in program and type RUN.
Press any key to throw dice.

```
100 REM Program P73 - Dice
110 MODE 7
120 @%=3
130 PRINT "This program rolls 3 dice. Note no"
140 PRINT "graphics. Press any key to throw the"
150 PRINT "dice"
160 Z=GET
170 REPEAT
180    D1=RND(6):D2=RND(6):D3=RND(6)
190    PRINT TAB(0,12) CHR$(141);CHR$(133);SPC(5),D1,D2,D3
200    PRINT TAB(0,13) CHR$(141);CHR$(133);SPC(5),D1,D2,D3
210    PRINT '''"Press any key for another throw"
220    Z=GET
230 UNTIL 0
```

P74   Pools Program

This program selects random numbers to help you fill up your football pools coupon.

I've not won yet!

COMMANDS

Key in program and type RUN
Follow instructions.

```
100 REM Program P74 - Pools Program
110 DIM temp%(100)
120 @%=3
130 CLS
140 PRINT ''''"This program will not win the pools"
150 PRINT "for you. It does not reduce the odds in"
160 PRINT "any way, but it does remove the"
170 PRINT "responsibility of losing from you."
180 PRINT "The program will present you with your"
190 PRINT "treble chance numbers"
200
210 INPUT ''"How many games on entry form",games
220 INPUT'"How many columns are you entering",columns
230 INPUT'"How many entries in each column",entries
240
250 CLS
260 FOR I=1 TO columns
270    FOR J=1 TO entries
280       temp%(J)=RND(games)
290       flag=0
300          FOR K=0 TO J-1
310             IF temp%(K)=temp%(J) THEN J=J-1:flag=1
320          NEXT K
330       IF flag=0 THEN PRINT TAB(I*5,J)temp%(J)
340    NEXT J
350 NEXT I
360 REM end of program
```

P75 Shuffle

It is important to be able to shuffle a deck of cards if you wish to write a card game program. There are three useful routines presented in this program.

1. A routine to set up a pack of cards (lines 120-290).
2. A shuffle routine (lines 310-370).
3. A routine to deal the cards (lines 380-470).

COMMANDS

Key in program and type RUN.


```
100 REM Program 75 - Shuffle
110 MODE 5
120 VDU 23,224,54,127,127,127,62,28,8,0
130 VDU 23,225,8,28,28,107,127,107,8,28
140 VDU 23,226,8,28,62,127,62,28,8,0
150 VDU 23,227,8,28,62,127,127,127,28,62
160 h$=CHR$(224)
170 c$=CHR$(225)
180 d$=CHR$(226)
190 s$=CHR$(227)
200 pack$=STRING$(104," "):pack$=""
210 heart$=STRING$(26," "):heart$=""
220 club$=STRING$(26," "):club$=""
230 diamond$=STRING$(26," "):diamond$=""
240 spade$=STRING$(26," "):spade$=""
250 hand1$=STRING$(26," "):hand1$=""
260 hand2$=STRING$(26," "):hand2$=""
270 hand3$=STRING$(26," "):hand3$=""
280 hand4$=STRING$(26," "):hand4$=""
290 heart$=FNsetup(heart$,h$)
300 club$=FNsetup(club$,c$)
310 diamond$=FNsetup(diamond$,d$)
320 spade$=FNsetup(spade$,s$)
330 pack$=heart$+club$+diamond$+spade$
340 PRINT TAB(5,10) "SHUFFLING"
350 shuffled$=pack$:shuffled$=""
360 FOR I=1 TO 50
370    P=RND(53-I)*2-1
380      shuffled$=shuffled$+ MID$(pack$,P,2)
390      pack$=LEFT$(pack$,P-1)+MID$(pack$,P+2)
400 NEXT I
410 shuffled$=shuffled$ + pack$
420 FOR I=1 TO 13
```

```
430    hand1$=hand1$+LEFT$(shuffled$,2)
440    shuffled$=MID$(shuffled$,3)
450    hand2$=hand2$+LEFT$(shuffled$,2)
460    shuffled$=MID$(shuffled$,3)
470    hand3$=hand3$+LEFT$(shuffled$,2)
480    shuffled$=MID$(shuffled$,3)
490    hand4$=hand4$+LEFT$(shuffled$,2)
500    shuffled$=MID$(shuffled$,3)
510 NEXT I
520 DIM X(4)
530 CLS
540 VDU 19,0,2;0;19,3,0;0;
550 PROCdeal(hand1$,3,0)
560 PROCdeal(hand2$,0,8)
570 PROCdeal(hand3$,8,16)
580 PROCdeal(hand4$,3,24)
590 END
600
610 DEF FNsetup(suit$,s$)
620    FOR I=2 TO 9
630       suit$=suit$+STR$(I)+s$
640    NEXT I
650    suit$="A"+s$+suit$+"T"+s$+"J"+s$+"Q"+s$+"K"+s$
660=suit$
670
680 DEF PROCdeal(nand$,X,R)
690   X(1)=X:X(2)=X:X(3)=X:X(4)=X
700   FOR I=1 TO 13
710     card$=MID$(hand$,I*2-1,2)
720     IF RIGHT$(card$,1)=h$ OR RIGHT$(card$,1)=d$
730     Y=ASC(RIGHT$(card$,1))-223
740     PRINT TAB(X(Y),Y+R)card$;
750     X(Y)=X(Y)+2
760   NEXT I
770 ENDPROC
```

P76 Number Base Conversion

This program is a very useful program for work in a computing lab. It allows the user to convert numbers from one base to another.

COMMANDS

Key in program and type RUN.
Select conversion required.

```
100 REM Program P76 - Number Base Conversion
110 MODE 7
120 PRINT TAB(12,12)"N U M B E R   B A S E"
130 PRINT TAB(13,14)"C O N V E R S I O N"
140 Z=INKEY(300)
150 REPEAT
160    CLS
170    PRINT '''"1. Hex to Decimal"
180    PRINT "2. Decimal to Hex"
190    PRINT "3. Octal to Decimal"
200    PRINT "4. Decimal to Octal"
210    PRINT "5. Binary to Decimal"
220    PRINT "6. Decimal to Binary"
230    INPUT '''"Enter appropriate choice "choice
240    ON choice GOSUB 290,450,510,640,750,890
          ELSE PRINT '''"Wrong choice - Try again"
250    PRINT '''''"Press key for another run"
260    Z=GET
270 UNTIL 0
280
290 CLS
300 PRINT '''"1. Hex to Decimal"
310 INPUT '''"Enter Hexadecimal Number - "hex$
320 dec%=0
330 index=0
340 REPEAT
350    digit$=RIGHT$(hex$,1)
360    d=ASC(digit$)
370    IF d>47 AND d<58 THEN d=d-48 ELSE
          IF d>64 AND d<71 THEN d=d-55 ELSE
            PRINT "Not Hex":RETURN
380    dec%=dec%+d*16^index
390    index=index+1
400    hex$=LEFT$(hex$,LEN(hex$)-1)
410 UNTIL LEN(hex$)=0
```

```
420 PRINT "Decimal is "dec%
430 RETURN
440
450 CLS
460 PRINT '''"2. Decimal to Hex"
470 INPUT '''"Enter Decimal Number - "dec%
480 PRINT "Hexadecimal is "~dec%
490 RETURN
500
510 CLS
520 PRINT '''"3. Octal to Decimal"
530 INPUT '''"Enter Octal Number - "oct%
540 dec%=0
550 index=0
560 REPEAT
570   dec%=dec%+(oct% MOD 10)*8^index
580   oct%=oct% DIV 10
590   index=index+1
600 UNTIL oct%=0
610 PRINT "Decimal is "dec%
620 RETURN
630
640 CLS
650 PRINT '''"4. Decimal to Octal"
660 INPUT '''"Enter Decimal Number - "dec%
670 oct$=""
680 REPEAT
690   oct$=STR$(dec% MOD 8) + oct$
700   dec%=dec% DIV 8
710 UNTIL dec%=0
720 PRINT "Octal is "oct$
730 RETURN
740
750 CLS
760 PRINT '''"5. Binary to Decimal"
770 INPUT '''"Enter Binary Number - "bin$
780 dec%=0
790 index=0
800 REPEAT
810   d=VAL(RIGHT$(bin$,1))
820   dec%=dec%+d*2^index
830   bin$=LEFT$(bin$,LEN(bin$)-1)
840   index=index+1
850 UNTIL LEN(bin$)=0
860 PRINT "Decimal is "dec%
870 RETURN
```

```
880
890 CLS
900 PRINT '''"6. Decimal to Binary"
910 INPUT ''"Enter Decimal Number - "dec%
920 bin$=""
930 REPEAT
940   bin$=STR$(dec% MOD 2)+bin$
950   dec%=dec% DIV 2
960 UNTIL dec%=0
970 PRINT "Binary is "bin$
980 RETURN
```

P77 Colour Codes For Resistors

This program could prove to be of great use in an electronics laboratory. It allows the user to calculate the value of a resistor from its colour code or to determine the colour code from its value.

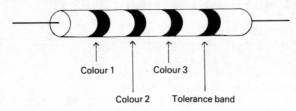

Colour 1   Colour 3

Colour 2   Tolerance band

COMMANDS

Key in program and type RUN.
Follow instructions.

```
100 REM Program P77 - Colour Codes For Resistors
110 CLS
120 PRINT TAB(0,7)"This program can be used to calculate"
130 PRINT "the value of a resistor from its colour"
140 PRINT "code or to calculate the code from its"
150 PRINT "value."
160 Z=INKEY(600)
170 DIM code$(9),colour$(3),val(3)
180 FOR I=0 TO 9
190    READ code$(I)
200 NEXT I
210 REPEAT
220    CLS
230    PRINT '"Do you wish to find value or code?"
240    PRINT "Enter 1 for value, 2 for code"
250    INPUT choice
260    IF choice=1 THEN PROCvalue ELSE
            IF choice=2 THEN PROCcode
270    INPUT "Another run (Y/N) "a$
280 UNTIL a$<>"y" AND a$<>"Y"
290 END
300 DATA BLACK,BROWN,RED,ORANGE,YELLOW,GREEN,BLUE,PURPLE,
        GREY,WHITE,EOD
310
320 DEF PROCvalue
330    CLS
340    @%=1
```

```
350    PRINT "COLOURS ARE :"'"BLACK"'"BROWN"'"RED"'"ORANGE"'
           "YELLOW"'"GREEN"'"BLUE"'"PURPLE"'"GREY"'"WHITE"
360    INPUT '"Colour 1", colour$(1)
370    INPUT "Colour 2", colour$(2)
380    INPUT "Colour 3", colour$(3)
390    FOR I=1 TO 3
400      FOR C=0 TO 9
410        IF code$(C)=colour$(I) THEN val(I)=C:C=9
420      NEXT C
430    NEXT I
440    PRINT "FOURTH BAND COLOURS ARE GOLD, SILVER OR"
450    PRINT "NONE"
460    INPUT "Tolerance band colour "tol$
470    IF tol$="GOLD" THEN tol$="5%" ELSE
           IF tol$="SILVER" THEN tol$="10%" ELSE tol$="20%"
480    PRINT ''"Value of resistor is "val(1);val(2)"*10^"
               val(3)" OHMS"
490   PRINT "Tolerance = "tol$
500  ENDPROC
510
520  DEF PROCcode
530    CLS
540    INPUT "What is resistor value?",value$
550    value=EVAL(value$)
560    l=LEN(STR$(INT(value)))
570    value=INT(value/(10^(l-2))+.5)
580    c1=value DIV 10
590    c2=value MOD 10
600    INPUT '"What tolerance do you require? (5,10 or  20%) "
               tol$
610    IF RIGHT$(tol$,1)<>"%" THEN tol$=tol$+"%"
620    IF tol$="5%" THEN tol$="GOLD" ELSE
           IF tol$="10%" THEN tol$="SILVER" ELSE tol$=" "
630   PRINT''"Colour code is"
640   PRINT code$(c1);" ";code$(c2);" ";code$(l-2);" ";tol$
650  ENDPROC
```

160

P78 Volumes of Solids

This program can be used to calculate the volumes of the following solids.

1. Sphere.

2. Cylinder.

3. Pyramid and Cone.

COMMAND

Key in program and type RUN.
Follow menus.

```
100 REM Program P78 - Volumes of Solids
110 REM This part of the program presents the main menu
120 REPEAT
130   CLS
140   PRINT'''"THIS PROGRAM CAN CALCULATE THE VOLUMES"
150   PRINT "OF THE FOLLOWING SOLIDS"''
160   PRINT''"1. SPHERE"
170   PRINT''"2. CYLINDER"
180   PRINT''"3. PYRAMID"
190   PRINT'''"Enter the  appropriate key value"
200   PRINT "for a particular choice, key 4 to"
210   PRINT "finish with program"
220   response=VAL(GET$):flag=0
```

```
230  ON response GOSUB 270,370,470:ELSE flag=1
240 UNTIL flag=1
250 CLS
260 END
270 REM This subroutine calculates the volume of a sphere
280 CLS
290 PRINT''"Calculating the volume of a sphere"
300 INPUT''"Enter the radius",r
310 volume=4*PI*r*r*r/3
320 PRINT''"Volume of sphere radius ";r;'"is ";volume
330 PRINT''"Press any key to return to main menu"''
340 A$=GET$
350 RETURN:REM end of subroutine
360
370 REM This subroutine calculates the volume of a cylinder
380 CLS
390 PRINT''"Calculating the volume of a cylinder"
400 INPUT''"Enter the base radius",r
410 INPUT "Enter the height",ht
420 volume=PI*r*r*ht
430 PRINT''"Volume of a cylinder"'"radius ";
         r,'"and height ";ht,'"is"''volume
440 PRINT''"Press any key to return to main menu"''
450 A$=GET$
460 RETURN:REM end of subroutine
470 REM This subroutine calculates the volume of
         a pyramid
480 CLS
490 PRINT'''"CALCULATION OF AREA OF CONE"
500 PRINT''"Do you know the base area(Y/N)";
510 a$=GET$
520 IF a$="Y" OR a$="y" THEN
     INPUT "Enter the base area",area
     ELSE PROCarea
530 INPUT'"Enter the height of the pyramid or cone",ht
540 volume=area*ht/3
550 PRINT'"Volume of pyramid with"'"base area=";
         area,'"and height=";ht,'"is"';volume
560 PRINT '"Press any key to return to the main menu"
570 A$=GET$
580 RETURN:REM end of subroutine
590
600 REM The following procedure calculates the
         base area of a pyramid or cone
610 DEF PROCarea
620    REPEAT
630       REM subsidiary menu to select base
640       CLS
```

```
650     PRINT'' "Select base shape by pressing"
660     PRINT "appropriate key"
670     PRINT' "1. Equilateral triangle"
680     PRINT' "2. Square"
690     PRINT' "3. Circle"
700     response=VAL(GET$)
710     flag_1=0
720     IF response=1 THEN
        INPUT' "Enter side",s:area=s*s*SIN(RAD(60))/2:
        flag_1=1
730     IF response=2 THEN
        INPUT' "Enter side",s:area=s*s:flag_1=1
740     IF response=3 THEN
        INPUT' "Enter radius",r:area=PI*r*r:flag_1=1
750    UNTIL flag_1=1
760 ENDPROC
770
780 REM End of program
```

P79 and P80 Physics

These two programs show how a micro could be used within a physics lab to take some of the drudgery out of experimentation.

The programs are based on two experiments in F. Tyler's "A Laboratory Manual Of Physics" (Edward Arnold 1966).

COMMAND

Use WORK SHEETS and programs to perform the experiments.

Work Sheet 1

Determination of the moment of inertia of a flywheel

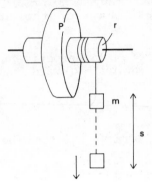

Apparatus

Wall supported flywheel of standard pattern. A weight is attached to a length of fine cord which is wrapped round the axle, the free end being passed through a hole in the axle. The length of the cord is adjusted so that when the weight reaches the ground, the cord detaches itself from the axle. Calipers, stop-watch, metre rule.

Method

The value of m is obtained by weighing, and the radius r of the axle found by using calipers.

The weight m is allowed to fall through a measured distance (s) to the ground, and the time of descent (t) is taken by a stop-watch. The number of revolutions (n) of the wheel during this time is taken by observing a mark made on the circumference of the wheel at P. The further revolutions (n) made by the wheel before coming to rest after m is detached are also counted by reference to the mark P. The experiment is repeated three times for the same distance (s).

Perform the experiment as follows:

      Power on microcomputer.
      Load program P79.
      Take measurements m,r and s.
      Run the program.
      Perform the experiment as directed, and enter values as prompted.

```
100 REM Program P79 - Moment of Inertia
110 MODE7
120 PRINT TAB(8,12) "Physics - Experiment 1"
130 PRINT TAB(4,14) "Moment of Inertia of a Flywheel"
140 Z=INKEY(300)
150 CLS
160 PRINT ''"SEE WORK SHEET!!!!"
170 PRINT ''"Input the following values"
180 INPUT '"Radius of axle (cm) "r
190 INPUT "Mass (g) "m
200 INPUT "Distance to the ground (cm) "s
210 g=981
220 PRINT ''"Perform experiment now"''
230 FOR I=1 TO 3
240 PRINT TAB(0,13)"RUN - "STR$(I)
250   INPUT TAB(0,15)"t(secs)= "t
260   INPUT "n(rev) = "n
270   INPUT "N(rev) = "N
280   tt=tt+t:nn=nn+n:NN=NN+N
290   PRINT TAB(0,15)STRING$(39," ");
300   PRINT TAB(0,16)STRING$(39," ");
310   PRINT TAB(0,17)STRING$(39," ");
320 NEXT I
330 t=tt/3
340 n=nn/3
350 N=NN/3
360 I=m*r*r*(g*t*t/2/s - 1)*(N/(N + n))
370 PRINT ''"Moment of inertia I =";I
380 END
```

Work Sheet 2

Apparatus

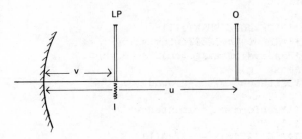

Concave mirror in stand, two retort stands with clamps and pins, metre rule.

Method

The object pin O is placed a given distance u from the concave mirror, and the position of the image I formed by reflection in the mirror is located by the method of non-parallax using the second pin (locating pin LP). The distance v of the locating pin from the mirror is measured. O and I are said to be conjugate points, and a series of values of v for a given range of values of u is obtained.

The computer program is used to calculate the focal length of the mirror from each measurement. The average of these values, and their standard deviation are calculated and presented on the screen.

```
100 REM Program P80 - Focal Length
110 MODE7
120 PRINT TAB(8,12) "Physics - Experiment 2"
130 PRINT TAB(4,14) "Determination of the focal length"
140 PRINT TAB(4,15) "of a concave mirror"
150 Z=INKEY(300)
160 CLS
170 PRINT ''"SEE WORK SHEET!!!!"
180 INPUT "How many measurements were taken "n
190 DIM f(n)
200 FOR I=1 TO n
210   PRINT "Measurement "STR$(I)
220   INPUT "u ="u
230   INPUT "v ="v
240   f(I)=1/(1/u+1/v)
250   sum=sum+f(I)
260   sum_sq=sum_sq + f(I)*f(I)
270   CLS
280 NEXT I
290
300 mean=sum/n
310 sdev=SQR(sum_sq/n - mean*mean)
320 PRINT "Average focal length= ";mean
330 PRINT "Standard Deviation =";sdev
340 END
```

P81 Resistors

This program computes the resultant resistance of an electric circuit of the following type:

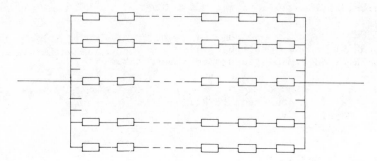

COMMANDS

Key in program and type RUN.
Follow instructions and enter resistances when required.

```
100 REM Program P81 - Resistors
110 MODE7
120 PRINT TAB(12,12)"R E S I S T O R S"
130 Z=INKEY(300)
140 CLS
150 PRINT '''"This program computes the resistance"
160 PRINT "in an electric circuit consisting"
170 PRINT "of branches of series resistors"
180 PRINT "connected in parallel"
190 INPUT '''"How many branches are there? ",branches
200 DIM res(branches)
210 @%=3
220 FOR I=1 TO branches
230   PRINT '"How many resistors in branch? "I;
240   INPUT resist
250   FOR J=1 TO resist
260     PRINT "What is the value of resistor? "J;
270     INPUT r
280     res(I)=res(I)+r
290   NEXT J
300   conductance=conductance+1/res(I)
310 NEXT I
320 @%=10
330 PRINT '''"TOTAL RESISTANCE ="1/conductance
340 END
```

P82 Calculator

There are many occasions when you need the capability of a simple calculator rather than a complex computer. This program simulates a simple four function (+,-,l,*) calculator.

When running the program notice that the appearance of the numbers is not quite the same as in the usual calculator. For example, if we add 111 to 123, the following happens:

User keys in	Screen Displays
1	1
2	12
3	123
+	123
1	124
1	134
1	234

COMMANDS

Key in program and type RUN.
Use numeric keys and (+,-,l,*) to perform arithmetic.
Use the full stop for the decimal point.

```
100 REM Program P82 - Calculator
110 MODE7
120 PRINT TAB(0,12)CHR$(141);CHR$(131)
130 PRINT TAB(0,13)CHR$(141);CHR$(131)
140 result$="."
150 PROCprint(result$)
160 a$="0"
170
180 REPEAT
190   i$=GET$
200   PRINT TAB(12,12) STRING$(20," ")
210   IF i$="*" OR i$="/" OR i$="+" OR i$="-"
220   IF (ASC(i$)>47 AND ASC(i$)<58)
230   IFi$="." THEN a$=a$+i$
240   PROCprint(result$)
250 UNTIL 0
260
270 DEF PROCprint(result$)
280   R$=STRING$(13-LEN(result$)," ")+result$
290   PRINT TAB(12,12)R$
300   PRINT TAB(12,13)R$
310 ENDPROC
```

P83 Coordinate Conversion

It can quite often happen that you have some points plotted on a graph in the rectangular (x,y) format, and you wish to convert this to the polar format (r,θ), as in the following figure:

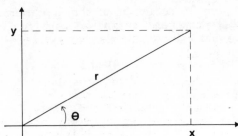

The conversion formulae are:
    x=r*cos(θ)
    y=r*sin(θ)
    r=SQR(x*x+y*y)
    θ=arc tan(y/x)

with slight variations for the various quadrants.

COMMANDS

Key in program and type RUN.
Follow instructions as presented on the screen.

```
100 REM Program P83 - Coordinate Conversion
110 REPEAT
120   CLS
130   PRINT "This program allows the user to convert"
140   PRINT "from rectangular to polar coordinates"
150   PRINT "and vice versa."
160
170   REM We initialise all variables used at this point,
         which is the main module of the program
180   x_coord=0:y_coord=0:r=0:theta=0
190   PRINT ''"Choose which conversion you want and"
200   PRINT "press the appropriate key"
210   PRINT'"1 for polar to rectangular"
220   PRINT'"2 for rectangular to polar"
230   PRINT'"any other to end."
240   keyin=VAL(GET$):flag=1
250   ON keyin GOSUB 290,460:ELSE flag=0
260 UNTIL flag=0
270 END
```

```
280
290 REM This subroutine converts  polar to rectangular
        coordinates
300 CLS
310 PRINT''"Enter the coordinates of your point in"
320 PRINT "the form r,theta"
330 INPUT r,theta
340 INPUT''"Is theta in degrees (Y/N)",answer$
350 IF LEFT$(answer$,1)="Y" OR LEFT$(answer$,1)="y"
    THEN theta=RAD(theta)
360
370 REM Notice the use of the RAD function
380 x_coord=r*COS(theta):y_coord=r*SIN(theta)
390 PRINT''"radial value=";r,"angle=";(DEG(theta))
400 PRINT''"x_coordinate=";x_coord,'"y_coordinate=";y_coord
410 PRINT''"Press any key to return to the main"
420 PRINT "module of the program"
430 A$=GET$:REM This line delays return
440 RETURN:REM end of subroutine
450
460 REM This  subroutine  converts rectangular  to polar
        coordinates,  with the option of the angle in
        degs or rads.
470 CLS
480 INPUT''"Enter the x_coordinate of your point"',x_coord
490 INPUT''"Enter the y_coordinate of your point"',y_coord
500 r=SQR(x_coord*x_coord+y_coord*y_coord)
510 IF x_coord=0 THEN
            theta=-RAD(90)*(y_coord>0)-RAD(270)*(y_coord<0)
520 IF x_coord<>0 THEN theta=ATN(y_coord/x_coord)+RAD(180)*
    (x_coord<0)*(y_coord<0) +RAD(180)*(x_coord<0)*(y_coord>0)+
    RAD(360)*(x_coord>0)*(y_coord<0)
530 INPUT''"Do you wish theta to be given in degrees(Y/N)?",
        answer$
540 IF LEFT$(answer$,1)="Y" OR LEFT$(answer$,1)="y"
    THEN theta=DEG(theta)
550 PRINT''"x_coordinate=";x_coord
560 PRINT"y_coordinate=";y_coord
570 PRINT''"radial value=";r,'"angle=";theta
580 PRINT''"Press any key to return to the main"
590 PRINT "module of the program"
600 A$=GET$:REM This line delays return
610 RETURN:REM end of subroutine
620 REM The end of the program
```

P84 Vectors

This is a rather simple program which could be used to find dot and cross products of vectors. The vectors used have only three components.

The program would have been more complex if it had been written for general vectors. However, I believe that this is a useful routine to have in any software library.

COMMANDS

Key in program and type RUN.
Enter vectors when prompted.

```
100 REM Program P84 - Vectors
110 MODE7
120 PRINT TAB(12,12)"V E C T O R "
130 PRINT TAB(4,14)"M U L T I P L I C A T I O N"
140 Z=INKEY(300)
150 CLS
160 PRINT "This program computes both the dot"
170 PRINT "and cross product of two vectors."
180 PRINT "The vectors are entered in component"
190 PRINT "form, and their products are then given."
200 PRINT "The vectors must be in 3D space"
210 DIM vector1(3),vector2(3),cross(3)
220 PRINT "Enter vector 1 "
230 FOR I=1 TO 3
240   INPUT vector1(I)
250 NEXT I
260 PRINT "Enter vector 2 "
270 FOR I=1 TO 3
280   INPUT vector2(I)
290 NEXT I
300 REM dot product
310 FOR I=1 TO 3
320   dot=dot+vector1(I)*vector2(I)
330 NEXT I
340 REM cross product
350 cross(1)=vector1(2)*vector2(3)-vector1(3)*vector2(2)
360 cross(2)=vector1(3)*vector2(1)-vector1(1)*vector2(3)
370 cross(3)=vector1(1)*vector2(2)-vector1(2)*vector2(1)
380
```

```
390 CLS
400 @%=5
410 PRINT "VECTOR 1 =" TAB(20)"VECTOR 2 =";
420 FOR I=1 TO 3
430   PRINT TAB(10,I-1) vector1(I); TAB(34,I-1)vector2(I);
440 NEXT I
450 PRINT ''"Dot Product is "dot
460 PRINT ''"Cross Product is ";
470 FOR I=1 TO 3
480   PRINT TAB(17,6+I) cross(I)
490 NEXT I
500 END
```

P85 Quadratic Equations

In this program we have to solve;

$$Ax*x + Bx + C = 0 \qquad\qquad (I)$$

To do this we use the formula;

$$x=-B \pm SQR(B*B - 4*A*C)/(2*A) \qquad\qquad (II)$$

This gives the two roots of (I). There are however, some problems:

1. If A=0, then we have division by zero in equation (II). But in this case the solution is trivial: x=C/B.
2. If B*B-4*A*C=0, then we only have one root x=-B/(2*A).
3. If B*B-4*A*C<0, then we have complex roots:

Note that because of roundoff errors, this algorithm is unsuitable for the case where B*B is very much greater than 4*A*C.

COMMANDS

Key in program and type RUN.
Enter coefficients in the correct order when prompted.

```
100 REM Program P85 - Quadratic Equations
190 CLS
200 PRINT "This  program solves  equations of the"
210 PRINT "form A*x*x + B*x + C = 0, thus you are"
220 PRINT "required to input the 3 parameters in"
230 PRINT "the correct order"
240
250 INPUT''"What is the coefficient of x*x?",A
260 INPUT''"What is the coefficient of x?",B
270 INPUT''"What is the constant term?",C
280
290 REM The next section of code catches the case of A=0
300
310 IF A=0 THEN PRINT ''"Solution to"'';
            B;"x+";C;"=0"''"is"
            ''"x=";(-C/B)'':END
320
```

```
330 REM Notice the use of the line feed character '
        and the ; to format the output
340 REM Once a solution has been calculated then
        the program ends
350
360 REM Before continuing we evaluate the discriminant
370
380 dis=B*B-4*A*C
390
400 IF dis=0 THEN PRINT '''"We have equal roots."''
                "The solution is x=";(-B/2/A)'':END
410 REM Again we use ' and ; to format the output
420
430 IF dis>0 THEN PRINT '''"We have 2 real roots"''
                "Root-1: x=";((-B+SQR(dis))/2/A)''
                "Root-2: x=";((-B-SQR(dis))/2/A)'':END
440
450 REM In the next section of code we format the output
        by using multiple print lines
460
470 PRINT '''"We have complex roots"
480 PRINT'''"Root-1 =";(-B/2/A);"+i*("(SQR(-dis)/2/A)")"
490 PRINT'''"Root-2 =";(-B/2/A);"-i*("(SQR(-dis)/2/A)")"''
500 END
```

P86 Factorisation

It is an interesting problem in mathematics that, given any whole number, we can find all its prime factors.

That is, given any positive integer N, we wish to express it as a product of powers of primes. Thus we wish to find all the primes P_i, and indices I_i such that

$$N = \sum P_i^{\wedge} I_i$$

For example:

$$180 = 2^2 * 3^2 * 5$$

We use a method of repeated division to find the set of factors of N.

Let us consider an example: find the prime factors of 180

The first possible factor of 180, is 2, and we can write

180=2*90

Now all the factors of 90 are contained in 180, so we need only consider the factors of 90.

180=2*2*45

Thus 2 is also a factor of 90, but 2 is not a factor of 45, because it does not divide evenly into 45, that is REMAINDER(45/2)$\neq$0

We can now try 3

180=2*2*3*15

and carrying on:

180=2*2*3*3*5

Thus

$$180 = 2^2 * 3^2 * 5$$

That, then, is the algorithm used by the program presented here. ·
Note that when the factors are presented, the first prime

is given as 1, this was just to aid the presentation of the result.

COMMANDS

Key in program and type RUN.
Enter number to be factorised.

```
100 REM Program P86 - Factorisation
110 CLS
120
130 PRINT''"This program can be used to factorise a"
140 PRINT "positive integer into its prime factors."
150 PRINT'"The  program,  at the  moment only uses"
160 PRINT "primes below 100"'''
170
180 dimension=100:REM This is tne line to amend to
                        increase the range of the program
190
200 DIM factor(dimension),indices(dimension)
210
220 INPUT "What number do you want factorised ",number
230
240 quotient=number
250
260 REM The following section of code finds the indices
270
280 FOR I=2 TO dimension
290    REPEAT
300      IF quotient MOD I=0 THEN factor(I)=1:
                           indices(I)=indices(I)+1:
                           quotient=quotient DIV I
310    UNTIL quotient MOD I<>0
320 NEXT I
330
340 REM If there is a 1 in the Ith position of the
          factor array then I is a factor of the
          number
350 REM and indices(I) is the index of that factor
360 REM The next section of code writes out the
          factorisation
370
380 PRINT '''"1";
390 FOR I=1 TO dimension
400    IF factor(I)=1 THEN PRINT ;"*";I;"^";indices(I);
410
420 NEXT I
430 PRINT''
440 END
```

P87 Factorial

In statistics we frequently wish to calculate expressions of the form

N*(N-1)*(N-2)*...*3*2*1

For example, if we want to know the number of ways of arranging the word COMPUTER, then :

we have 8 ways of choosing the first letter
we have 7 ways of choosing the second letter
we have 6 ways of choosing the third letter
and so on

Thus, in total, we have

8*7*6*5*4*3*2*1=40320

ways of arranging the word COMPUTER.
Such objects are known as factorials and are defined as follows

N!=N*(N-1)*(N-2)*....*3*2*1

where ! is the symbol for factorial.

A more elegant definition of factorial is:

$$N! = \begin{cases} N*(N-1)! & , N>1 \\ 1 & , N=1. \end{cases}$$

It is this definition which is used in the following program.

Note that the largest factorial possible using this program is 33!, this is due to the way numbers are stored in computers.

COMMANDS

Key in program and type RUN.
Follow instructions.

```
100 REM Program P87 - Factorial
110 MODE4
120 PRINT "This program can be used to evaluate"
130 PRINT "the factorial of a number."
140 PRINT'"The program uses the formula :"
150  PRINT '"   N!={ 1 , if N=1 "
160  PRINT  "        { N*(N-1)!, otherwise"
170 PRINT'"Because of the limited range of numbers"
180 PRINT "in computers, the largest factorial"
190 PRINT "possible is 33!"
200 REPEAT
210   INPUT'"What is the number?",number
215   number=INT(number)
220   IF number>33 THEN PRINT'"Number is too large":GOTO 260
225   IF number<1 THEN PRINT'"Number is too small":GOTO 260
230   PRINT''number"! = "FNfactorial(number)
240   PRINT''"Do you wish to evaluate another"'
               "factorial?";:INPUT answer$
250   a$=LEFT$(answer$,1)
260 UNTIL a$<>"Y" AND a$<>"y"
270 END
280 DEF FNfactorial(x)
290   IF x>33 THEN =0
295   IF x<1 THEN =0
300   IF x=1 THEN result=1 ELSE result=x*FNfactorial(x-1)
310   =result
```

P88 Polynomial Multiplication

This is a rather useful routine when working with polynomials. The program allows the user to multiply two polynomials together, taking all the hard work out of it.

EXAMPLE

Multiply (2*x*x+3*x+2) by x+1

If this has to be performed by hand, we proceed as follows;

$$
\begin{array}{r}
2x^2 + 3x + 2 \\
x + 1 \\
\hline
2x^2 + 3x + 2 \\
2x^3 + 3x^2 + 2x \\
\hline
2x^3 + 5x^2 + 5x + 2 \\
\hline
\end{array}
$$

This can be a rather time consuming exercise when the polynomials become large. This program does all the work for you.

The BBC micro, in common with most others, cannot express polynomials in a very satisfying manner, but bear with this, and the algorithm can be very useful.

COMMANDS

Key in program and type RUN.
Follow instructions, keying in parameters as prompted.

```
100 REM Program P88 - Polynomial Multiplication
110 MODE 7
120 DIM a(20),b(20),c(40)
130 PRINT TAB(12,12)"P O L Y N O M I A L "
140 PRINT TAB(8,14)"M U L T I P L I C A T I O N"
150 Z=INKEY(300)
160 CLS
170 PRINT "This program can be used to find the "
180 PRINT "result of multiplying two polynomials"
190 PRINT "together."
200 PRINT '"The polynomials are of the form"
210 PRINT '"P(x)=a(0)x^0+a(1)x^1+a(2)x^2...a(n)x^n"
220 PRINT "Q(x)=b(0)x^0+b(1)x^1+b(2)x^2...b(m)x^m"
```

```
230 PRINT '"and the result is"
240 PRINT '"P(x).Q(x)="
250 PRINT "c(0)x^0+c(1)x^1+c(2)x^2...c(m+n)x^(m+n)"
260 PRINT ''"You are only required to enter the"
270 PRINT "degree of each polynomial and their"
280 PRINT "coefficients."
290 PRINT '''"Hit any key to continue"
300 Z=GET
310 CLS
320 @%=2
330 INPUT ''"Enter degree of polynomial 1 "n
340 FOR I=0 TO n
350   PRINT "coefficient "I"=";
360   INPUT a(I)
370 NEXT I
380
390 INPUT ''"Enter degree of polynomial 2 "m
400 FOR J=0 TO m
410   PRINT"coefficient "J"=";
420   INPUT b(J)
430 NEXT J
440 @%=10
450 Z=INKEY(10)
460 FOR K=0 TO n+m:c(K)=0:NEXT K
470 FOR I=0 TO n
480   FOR J=0 TO m
490     c(J+I)=c(J+I)+b(J)*a(I)
500   NEXT J
510 NEXT I
520 CLS
530 @%=3
540 PRINT "The result of multiplying"''
550 FOR I=0 TO n
560   PRINT a(I)"*x^"STR$(I)"+";
570 NEXT I
580 PRINT CHR$(127)
590 PRINT "by"
600 FOR J=0 TO m
610   PRINT b(J)"*x^"STR$(J)"+";
620 NEXT J
630 PRINT CHR$(127)
640 PRINT '"is"
650 FOR K=0 TO n+m
660   PRINT c(K)"*x^"STR$(K)"+";
670 NEXT K
680 PRINT CHR$(127)
690 END
```

, PFBM: G

P89 Jacobi Method for Solving Systems of Equations

The problem of solving systems of linear equations is one which arises in many branches of science, for example:

> *Numerical Solution of Partial Differential Equations
> *Least Squares Approximations
> *Current Flow Problems.

A system of linear equations is a set of equations with many unknowns. In school we met systems of three equations in three unknowns, for example:

$$3x+2y-z=4$$
$$x+3y+z=10$$
$$-2x-2y+4z=6$$

In school, this would be solved by elimination, giving the result $x=1, y=2, z=3$.

However, the method of elimination is not appropriate for solving large scale problems with a computer. This is because of the errors generated by using approximations to the results of arithmetic calculations.

In this program we use an iterative method of solving such systems of equations. After inputting the various parameters of the problem, the program requests that you input an initial approximation to the solution vector. The program improves this solution iteratively until it is within a desired accuracy of solution.

For the purpose of the program, we consider the system of equations to be written in the form

$Ax=b$

Where A is the matrix of coefficients of the system of equations, and b is the vector of the RHS of the equations.

COMMANDS

Key in program and type RUN.
Follow instructions.

```
100 REM Program P89 - Jacobi Method for Solving
                      Systems of Equations
110 REM Main program module.
120 CLEAR:REM Clears all variables
130 CLS  : REM Clear screen
140 PRINT ''"This program uses the Jacobi method for"
150 PRINT "solving a system of linear equations."
160 PRINT ''"Please enter the dimension of the system"
170 INPUT Dimension
180 PROCinitialise
190 REPEAT
200    PROCinputmatrix
210    INPUT''"Is this OK",Answer$
220 UNTIL LEFT$(Answer$,1)="Y" OR LEFT$(Answer$,1)="y"
230 REPEAT
240    PROCinputvector
250    INPUT''"Is this OK",Answer$
260 UNTIL LEFT$(Answer$,1)="Y" OR LEFT$(Answer$,1)="y"
270 PROCsolutionpossible
280 IF Nosolution THEN STOP
290 INPUT'"Enter desired accuracy of solution",Accuracy
300 REPEAT
310 PROCinitialapprox
320    INPUT''"Is this OK",Answer$
330 UNTIL LEFT$(Answer$,1)="Y" OR LEFT$(Answer$,1)="y"
340 REPEAT
350    PROCJacobi
360    PROCaccuracycheck
370    Iteration=Iteration+1
380 UNTIL Error<Accuracy
390 CLS
400 PRINT ''"The solution using the Jacobi method is"''
410 PRINT "X="
420 FOR Row=1 TO Dimension
430    PRINT Solution(Row)
440 NEXT Row
450 PRINT''"Number of iterations= ";Iteration
460 PRINT''"Type RUN for another go"
470 END
480
490
500 DEF PROCinitialise
510 @%=&A0A
520 DIM Coefft(Dimension,Dimension),Vector(Dimension),
        Solution(Dimension),Oldsoln(Dimension)
```

```
530 Accuracy=0:Rowsum=0:Error=0
540 Iteration=0:Nosolution=0
550 PRINT "What  is the max. no of digits in your"
        '"matrix element values? ";:INPUT Max
560 ENDPROC
570
580
590 DEF PROCinputmatrix
600 CLS
610 PRINT ''"Please enter the components of the"
620 PRINT "coefficient matrix element by element,"
630 PRINT "row-wise"''
640 PRINT "Note that matrix should be diagonally"
650 PRINT "dominant."
660 FOR Row=1 TO Dimension
670   PRINT '"Row - ";Row
680   FOR Column=1 TO Dimension
690     INPUT Coefft(Row,Column)
700   NEXT Column
710 NEXT Row
720 CLS
730 PRINT''"Coefficient matrix is"''
740 FOR Row=1 TO Dimension
750   FOR Column=1 TO Dimension
760     PRINT Coefft(Row,Column);
770   NEXT Column
780   PRINT
790 NEXT Row
800 ENDPROC
810
820
830 DEF PROCinputvector
840 CLS
850 PRINT ''"Please enter the components of the"
860 PRINT "righthand side vector B"
870 FOR Element=1 TO Dimension
880   INPUT Vector(Element)
890 NEXT Element
900 CLS
910 PRINT ''"Vector is "''
920 FOR Element =1 TO Dimension
930   PRINT Vector(Element)
940 NEXT Element
950 ENDPROC
960
970
```

```
 980 DEF PROCsolutionpossible
 990 FOR Diag=1 TO Dimension
1000   IF Coefft(Diag,Diag)=0 THEN
           PRINT "NO SOLUTION": Nosolution=1
1010 NEXT Diag
1020 ENDPROC
1030 DEF PROCinitialapprox
1040   CLS
1050 PRINT ''"Please enter your initial approximation"
1060 PRINT "element by element"
1070 FOR Element=1 TO Dimension
1080   INPUT Oldsoln(Element)
1090 NEXT Element
1100 CLS
1110 PRINT''"Approximation is"''
1120 FOR Element =1 TO Dimension
1130   PRINT Oldsoln(Element)
1140 NEXT Element
1150 ENDPROC
1160
1170
1180 DEF PROCJacobi
1190 FOR Row =1 TO Dimension
1200   Rowsum=0
1210   FOR Column=1 TO Dimension
1220      IF NOT (Row=Column) THEN
           Rowsum=Rowsum +
                Coefft(Row,Column)*Oldsoln(Column)
1230   NEXT Column
1240   Solution(Row)=(Vector(Row)-Rowsum)/Coefft(Row,Row)
1250 NEXT Row
1260 ENDPROC
1270
1280
1290 DEF PROCaccuracycheck
1300 Error=0
1310 FOR Element=1 TO Dimension
1320   Error=Error+(Oldsoln(Element)-Solution(Element))^2
1330 NEXT Element
1340 Error=SQR(Error)
1350 FOR Element=1 TO Dimension
1360   Oldsoln(Element)=Solution(Element)
1370 NEXT Element
1380 ENDPROC
```

P90 Greatest Common Divisor

This program uses the Euclidean Algorithm to compute the
greatest common divisor of two natural numbers.

COMMANDS

Key in program and type RUN.
Enter numbers as positive integers.

```
100 REM Program P90 - Greatest Common Divisor
110 MODE 7
120 PRINT ''"This program uses the Euclidean"
130 PRINT "Algorithm to compute the greatest"
140 PRINT "common divisor of two natural numbers."
150 INPUT ''"Enter first number "X1%
            "Enter second number " X2%
160 A%=X1%:B%=X2%
170 IF A%<B% THEN T%=B%:B%=A%:A%=T%
180 REM A is the larger number
190
200 REPEAT
210   remainder=A% MOD B%
220   quotient=A% DIV B%
230   A%=B%
240   B%=remainder
250 UNTIL remainder=0
260
270 PRINT '''"The greatest common divisor of"'''
280 PRINT STR$(X1%) " and " STR$(X2%) " is " STR$(A%)
290 END
```

```
This program uses the Euclidean
Algorithm to compute the greatest
common divisor of two natural numbers
Enter first number 72
Enter second number 20
The greatest common divisor of
72 and 20 is 4
```

P91 Matrix Multiplication

This program takes the tedium out of multiplying two matrices together. Notice that the program ensures that the multiplication is possible before carrying it out.

Note that the layout of fairly large matrices is not very good due to the limitations of the computer's display.

COMMANDS

Key in program and type RUN.
Enter dimensions of matrices in the form X*Y, e.g. 2*3.
Enter components of matrices when prompted.

```
100 REM Program P91 - Matrix Multiplication
110 MODE 7
120 PRINT "MATRIX MULTIPLICATION"
130 REPEAT
140    INPUT''"Dimension matrix A " dimA$
150    X=INSTR(dimA$,"*")
160 UNTIL X<>0
170 N=VAL(LEFT$(dimA$,X-1))
180 M=VAL(MID$(dimA$,X+1))
190 REPEAT
200    INPUT''"Dimension matrix B " dimB$
210    X=INSTR(dimB$,"*")
220 UNTIL X<>0
230 P=VAL(LEFT$(dimB$,X-1))
240 Q=VAL(MID$(dimB$,X+1))
250 IF M<>P THEN PRINT "CANNOT BE DONE!!!!":END
260 DIM A(N,M),B(P,Q),C(N,Q)
270 REM Input matrix A
280 FOR I=1 TO N
290    FOR J=1 TO M
300       PRINT "A("STR$(I)","STR$(J)")=";
310       INPUT A(I,J)
320    NEXT J
330 NEXT I
340 FOR I=1 TO P
350    FOR J=1 TO Q
360       PRINT "B("STR$(I)","STR$(J)")=";
370       INPUT B(I,J)
380    NEXT J
390 NEXT I
400
```

```
410 FOR I=1 TO N
420   FOR J=1 TO Q
430     FOR K=1 TO M
440       C(I,J)=C(I,J)+A(I,K)*B(K,J)
450     NEXT K
460   NEXT J
470 NEXT I
480
490 CLS
500 FOR I=1 TO N
510   PRINT "ROW "STR$(I)
520   FOR J=1 TO Q
530     PRINT C(I,J);
540   NEXT J
550   PRINT
560 NEXT I
570 END
```

P92 Secant Method

This program can be used to find a root of a function of a single variable. The secant method can be interpreted geometrically as follows.

Consider the diagram.

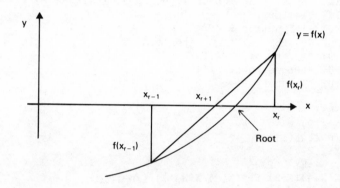

If x_r and x_{r-1} lie on either side of a root, then we can draw the secant between the points $(x_{r-1}, f(x_{r-1}))$ and $(x_r, f(x_r))$. The secant cuts the x-axis at the point x_{r+1}. Let x_{r+1} be the new approximation, then by similar triangles

$$\frac{x_{r+1} - x_{r-1}}{-f(x_{r-1})} = \frac{x_r - x_{r+1}}{f(x_r)}$$

$$\therefore \quad x_{r+1} = x_r - f(x_r) \frac{(x_r - x_{r-1})}{f(x_r) - f(x_{r-1})}$$

The same relationship can be formed even if both approximations lie on the same side of the root.

COMMANDS

Key in program and type RUN.
Enter function and two initial approximations when required.
Enter accuracy when prompted.

PFBM-G*

```
100 REM Program P92 - Secant Method
110 ON ERROR
        PRINT "TRY AGAIN WITH DIFFERENT INITIAL VALS":
        REPORT:END
120 MODE 7
130 PRINT "Finding a root to an equation using the"
140 PRINT "Secant Method"
150 PRINT "Enter function of X, using capital "
160 PRINT "letters."'
170 INPUT ''"Function = "f$
180 DIM X(40):REM max of 40 iterates
190 INPUT "First point "X(0)
200 INPUT "Second point "X(1)
210 INPUT "Accuracy "acc
220 R=1
230 REPEAT
240    X=X(R)
250    fr=EVAL(f$)
260    X=X(R-1)
270    fr_1=EVAL(f$)
280    X(R+1)=X(R)-fr*(X(R)-X(R-1))/(fr-fr_1)
290    R=R+1
300 UNTIL R=40 OR ABS(X(R)-X(R-1))<acc
310 PRINT "Root is "X(R)" at the "STR$(R)"'th iterate"
320 END
```

```
        Finding a root to an equation using the
        Secant Method
        Function = SIN(X)
        First point -.1
        Second point .1
        Accuracy 1E-10
        Root is -4.85630281E-14 at the 3'th iterate
```

P93 Method of Bisections

The method of bisections is based on the use of sign changes to find a root of a function.

Consider the following diagram.

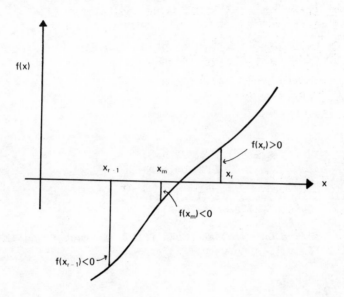

If we have two points x_r, x_{r-1}, for which $f(x_r)$ and $f(x_{r-1})$ have opposite signs, then there is a root between x_r and x_{r-1}. We can then evaluate $f(x)$ at the mid point between x_r and x_{r-1}, x_m, say. If $f(x_m)=0$ then we have a root. If $SGN(f(x_m))$ is the opposite to that of $f(x_{r-1})$, then the root lies between x_{r-1} and x_m. Otherwise the root lies between x_m and x_r.

That is the idea of the method of bisections, which is used in this program.

COMMANDS

Key in program and type RUN.
Enter function when prompted.
Enter end points of interval straddling root when prompted.
Enter accuracy desired.

```
100 REM Program P93 - Method of Bisections
110 ON ERROR
        PRINT "TRY AGAIN WITH DIFFERENT INITIAL VALS":
        REPORT:END
120 MODE7
130 PRINT "Finding a root to an equation using the"
140 PRINT "method of bisections"
150 INPUT ''"Function = "f$
160 f$=FNcase(f$)
170 INPUT "End point 1 = "ep1:a=ep1
180 INPUT "End point 2 = "ep2:b=ep2
190 INPUT "Accuracy = "acc
200 REPEAT
210   X=(a+b)/2
220   f1=EVAL(f$)
230   X=a
240   fa=EVAL(f$)
250   IF SGN(f1)=SGN(fa) THEN a=(a+b)/2
                             ELSE b=(a+b)/2
260   X=(a+b)/2
270 UNTIL EVAL(f$)=0 OR ABS(b-a)<acc
280 d_ep1=SQR((ep1-a)^2+(ep1-b)^2)
290 d_ep2=SQR((ep2-a)^2+(ep2-b)^2)
300 IF d_ep2<acc OR d_ep1<acc THEN PRINT "No root found":END
310 PRINT "Root lies between "'a'"and"'b
320 END
330 DEF FNcase(a$)
340   LOCAL d$,I,c$,c
350   d$=""
360   FOR I=1 TO LEN(a$)
370     c$=MID$(a$,I,1)
380     c=ASC(c$)
390     IF c>96 AND c<122 THEN c$=CHR$(c-32)
400     d$=d$+c$
410   NEXT I
420=d$
```

```
Finding a root to an equation using the
method of Bisections
Function = SIN(X)
End point 1 = -.1
End point 2 = .1
Accuracy = 1E-10
Root lies between
-3.7252903E-10
and
            0
```

P94 Trapezoidal Rule

This program uses the trapezoidal rule to evaluate a definite integral, of the form

$$I = \int_a^b f(x)$$

Thus the program requires as input:

    $f(x)$
    a and b

A definite integral can be considered to be the area under the graph of a function. The trapezoidal rule approximates this area by a series of trapeziums as in the following diagram.

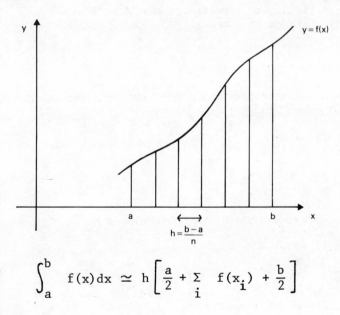

$$\int_a^b f(x)\,dx \simeq h\left[\frac{a}{2} + \sum_i f(x_i) + \frac{b}{2}\right]$$

COMMANDS

Key in program and type RUN.
Enter details as prompted.

```
100 REM Program P94 - Trapezoidal Rule
110 CLS
120 INPUT "Function to be integrated",function$
130 INPUT "Value of a",a,"Value of b",b
140 INPUT "Number of points",n
150
160 h=(b-a)/n
170 X=a
180 low_end_term=(EVAL(function$))/2
190 X=b
200 high_end_term=(EVAL(function$))/2
210 X=a
220 A=0
230 FOR I=1 TO n-1
240    X=X+h
250    A=A+EVAL(function$)
260 NEXT I
270 integral=(low_end_term+A+high_end_term)*h
280 PRINT "Integral=" integral
```

P95 Simpson's Rule

Simpson's Rule is a little bit more complicated algorithm than the trapezoidal rule. In Simpson's Rule we use a quadratic curve between the end points of the interval rather than a straight line. This leads to the following rule.

$$\int_a^b f(x)\,dx \simeq \frac{h}{3}\Big[f(x_0) + 4f(x_1) + 2f(x_2) + 4f(x_3)$$

$$+ 2f(x_4) + \ldots + f(x_n)\Big]$$

where $x_0 = a$, $x_n = b$ (n is even), $x_i = a + i * h$.

COMMANDS

Key in program and type RUN.
Enter function, a and b when prompted.
Enter number of points.
Note that if you enter an odd number, then 1 will be added.

```
100 REM Program P95 - Simpson's Rule
110 CLS
120 INPUT "Function to be integrated", function$
130 INPUT "Value of a",a,"Value of b",b
140 INPUT "Value of n, must be even",n
150 IF n MOD 2=1 THEN n=n+1:
       PRINT "Have added 1 to n to make it even"
160 h=(b-a)/n
170 X=a
180 first_value=EVAL(function$)
190 X=b
200 last_value=EVAL(function$)
210 X=a:even_vals=0:odd_vals=0
220 FOR I=1 TO n-3 STEP 2
230     X=X+h
240     odd_vals=odd_vals + EVAL(function$)
250     X=X+h
260     even_vals=even_vals + EVAL(function$)
270 NEXT I
280 X=X+h
290 odd_vals=odd_vals + EVAL(function$)
300 integral=(first_value+last_value+
                4*odd_vals+2*even_vals)*h/3
310 PRINT "Integral= "integral
```

P96 Arithmetic Tutor

This is the bare bones of a tutorial program which could be
used in a primary school class. The program allows the pupil
to have practice in simple arithmetic problems. The program
is constructed in such a way as to allow the pupil to enter
the answer in a natural manner. For example, if we have the
following sum:

```
    123
  + 25
  ─────
```

The pupil will enter the answer by pressing key 8 then key 4
then key 1 then (RETURN) to complete the answer.

COMMANDS

Key in program and type RUN.
Select problem type.
Enter result then press RETURN.
If correct main menu is displayed.
If wrong, enter new answer.

```
100 REM Program P96 - Arithmetic Tutor
110 MODE 7
120 PRINT TAB(12,12)"A R I T H M E T I C"
130 PRINT TAB(14,14)"  T U T O R"
140 Z=INKEY(300)
150 REPEAT
160    CLS
170    PRINT "You will be presented with an"
180    PRINT "arithmetic problem. Solve the problem"
190    PRINT "by keying in your solution in the"
200    PRINT "normal manner."
210    PRINT '"Problems can be given in:"
220    PRINT '"1. Addition"
230    PRINT "2. Subtraction"
240    PRINT "3. Division"
250    PRINT "4. Multiplication"
260    INPUT '"Make your choice "choice%
270    ON choice% GOSUB 580,670,760,1040
280    INPUT ''''"Another run",resp$
290 UNTIL LEFT$(resp$,1)<>"Y"
300 END
310
```

```
320 DEF PROCproblem(s$,result)
330 n1$=STR$(num1)
340 n2$=STR$(num2)
350 PRINT TAB(0,12) CHR$(141);CHR$(129);SPC(20-LEN(n1$));n1$;
360 PRINT TAB(0,13) CHR$(141);CHR$(129);SPC(20-LEN(n1$));n1$;
370 PRINT TAB(0,15) CHR$(141);CHR$(129);SPC(18-LEN(n2$));s$;n2$;
380 PRINT TAB(0,16) CHR$(141);CHR$(129);SPC(18-LEN(n2$));s$;n2$;
390 PRINT TAB(17,18) STRING$(5,"_")
400 REPEAT
410   b$=""
420   P=21
430   PRINT TAB(0,19) CHR$(141);CHR$(129)
440   PRINT TAB(0,20) CHR$(141);CHR$(129)
450   REPEAT
460     correct=FALSE
470     a$=GET$
480     IF ASC(a$)<>13 THEN b$=a$+b$:
        PRINT TAB(P,19)a$;:PRINT TAB(P,20)a$:P=P-1
490   UNTIL ASC(a$)=13
500   IF VAL(b$)=result THEN PRINT TAB(5,22)"CORRECT - WELL DONE'
      :correct=TRUE ELSE PRINT TAB(5,22) "WRONG - TRY AGAIN"
510   Z=INKEY(300)
520   PRINT TAB(5,19) STRING$(20," ")
530   PRINT TAB(5,20) STRING$(20," ")
540 UNTIL correct
550 ENDPROC
560
570
580 REM Addition
590 num1=RND(999)
600 num2=RND(999)
610 CLS
620 PRINT '''"        A D D I T I O N"
630 PROCproblem("+ ",num1+num2)
640 RETURN
650
660
670 REM Subtraction
680 num1=RND(999)
690 num2=RND(num1)
700 CLS
710 PRINT '''"        S U B T R A C T I O N"
720 PROCproblem("- ",num1-num2)
730 RETURN
740
750
```

```
 760 REM Division
 770 CLS
 780 REPEAT
 790 num2=RND(9)
 800 num1=RND(99)*num2
 810 UNTIL INT(num1/num2)=num1/num2
 820 PRINT '''"       D I V I S I O N"
 830 n1$=STR$(num1)
 840 n2$=STR$(num2)
 850 PRINT TAB(10,12)CHR$(141);CHR$(129);n2$;CHR$(151);
                     CHR$(181);CHR$(129);n1$
 860 PRINT TAB(10,13)CHR$(141);CHR$(129);n2$;CHR$(151);
                     CHR$(181);CHR$(129);n1$
 870 PRINT TAB(13,14)CHR$(151);CHR$(245);STRING$(5,CHR$(240))
 880 REPEAT
 890   b$=""
 900   P=16
 910   PRINT TAB(0,17) CHR$(141);CHR$(129)
 920   PRINT TAB(0,18) CHR$(141);CHR$(129)
 930   REPEAT
 940     correct=FALSE
 950     a$=GET$
 960     IF ASC(a$)<>13 THEN b$=b$+a$:PRINT TAB(P,17)a$;:
            PRINT TAB(P,18)a$:P=P+1
 970   UNTIL ASC(a$)=13
 980   IF VAL(b$)=num1/num2 THEN
         PRINT TAB(5,22)"CORRECT - WELL DONE":correct=TRUE
       ELSE PRINT TAB(5,22) "WRONG - TRY AGAIN"
 990   Z=INKEY(300)
1000   PRINT TAB(5,17) STRING$(20," ");
1010   PRINT TAB(5,18) STRING$(20," ");
1020   PRINT TAB(5,22) STRING$(20," ");
1030 UNTIL correct
1040 RETURN
1050
1060
1070 REM Multiplication
1080 CLS
1090 num1=RND(999)
1100 num2=RND(9)
1110 PRINT '''"      M U L T I P L I C A T I O N"
1120 PROCproblem("* ",num1*num2)
1130 RETURN
```

P97 and P98 French and German Tutorial

These are two implementations of a language vocabulary
tutorial. In both cases, the data is in the form of word
pairs starting at line 410. The teacher would insert his own
vocabulary starting at line 410.

The program gives the student up to three attempts at each
word, and after the tutorial is finished, some statistics
are returned.

COMMANDS

Key in program(s) and type RUN.
Follow instructions.

```
100 REM Program P97 - French Tutorial
110 DIM results(4)
120 @%=2
130 CLS
140 PRINT TAB(10,12) CHR$(141);"FRENCH TUTORIAL"
150 PRINT TAB(10,13) CHR$(141);"FRENCH TUTORIAL"
160 X=INKEY(300)
170 RESTORE
180
190 REPEAT
200    attempt=1
210    READ english$,french$
220    REPEAT
230      CLS
240      PRINT ''''''
250      PRINT "Attempt number "attempt
260      PRINT ''"English word is "english$
270      INPUT ''"What is the French "answer$
280      attempt=attempt+1
290    UNTIL answer$=french$ OR attempt=4
300    IF answer$<>french$ THEN results(4)=results(4)+1
       ELSE results(attempt-1)=results(attempt-1)+1
310 UNTIL english$="end"
320
330 CLS
340 PRINT '''
350 PRINT "Number correct at first attempt is " results(1)
360 PRINT ''"Number correct at second attempt is " results(2)
370 PRINT ''"Number correct at third attempt is " results(3)
380 PRINT  ''"Number of unknown answers" results(4)
390
400
410 DATA yes,oui,no,non,end,"fin"
```

```
100 REM Program 98 - German Tutorial
110 DIM results(4)
120 @%=2
130 CLS
140 PRINT TAB(10,12) CHR$(141);"GERMAN TUTORIAL"
150 PRINT TAB(10,13) CHR$(141);"GERMAN TUTORIAL"
160 X=INKEY(300)
170 RESTORE
180
190 REPEAT
200    attempt=1
210    READ english$,german$
220    REPEAT
230      CLS
240      PRINT ''''''
250      PRINT "Attempt number "attempt
260      PRINT ''"English word is "english$
270      INPUT ''"What is the German "answer$
280      attempt=attempt+1
290    UNTIL answer$=german$ OR attempt=4
300    IF answer$<>german$ THEN results(4)=results(4)+1
       ELSE results(attempt-1)=results(attempt-1)+1
310 UNTIL english$="end"
320
330 CLS
340 PRINT '''
350 PRINT "Number correct at first attempt is " results(1)
360 PRINT ''"Number correct at second attempt is " results(2)
370 PRINT ''"Number correct at third attempt is " results(3)
380 PRINT  ''"Number of unknown answers" results(4)
390
400
410 DATA yes,ja,no,nein,end,"Ende"
```

P99 Spelling

This program can be used as a spelling aid for young children. The instructions for using the program are included with it.

The idea of this program is to give a positive feedback to the pupil by making a game out of spelling. The teacher can change the vocabulary by replacing the data at line 960. If more than six words are required, then change line 370.

This program could be developed as a teaching package, by including an instruction to teacher section, and a report section.

COMMANDS

Key in program and type RUN.
Enter difficulty (1-9), 1 is hardest.
Note word when it appears.
Use key <SHIFTLOCK> to move gun left.
Use key <DELETE> to move gun right.
Use key 0 to fire.

```
100 REM Program P99 - Spelling
110 MODE 7
120 PRINT '''"This program can be used as a spelling"
130 PRINT "aid for young children. The user will"
140 PRINT "see the word for 6 seconds then he or"
150 PRINT "she has to shoot the letters of the"
160 PRINT "word from an alphabet at the top of the"
170 PRINT "screen. If the word is spelled"
180 PRINT "correctly a spaceship will cross the"
190 PRINT "screen, to be shot down by the user."
200 PRINT '''"Points are scored for each correct"
210 PRINT "letter, and for shooting down the"
220 PRINT "spaceship."
230 INPUT '''"Enter difficulty (1 to 9)" d
240 z=INKEY(100)
250
260 MODE 4
270 @%=4
280 VDU 19,0,4,0,0,0
290 VDU 23,224,0,60,126,171,255,126,36,36
300 VDU 23,225,24,24,24,24,24,255,255,255
310 VDU 23,226,24,24,24,24,24,24,24,24
320 VDU 23;8202;0;0;0
```

```
330 PRINT "        abcdefghijklmnopqrstuvwxyz"
340 PRINT TAB(16,30) "SCORE-"
350 X=20:Y=d*3
360
370 FOR K=1 TO 6
380    READ word$
390    PRINT TAB(1,16)word$
400    z=INKEY(600)
410    PRINT TAB(1,16) STRING$(40," ")
420    PRINT TAB(X,Y) CHR$(225);
430    flag=TRUE
440    REPEAT
450      DX=INKEY(-81)-INKEY(-90)
460      PRINT TAB(X,Y)" ";
470      X=ABS((X+DX) MOD 39)
480      PRINT TAB(X,Y) CHR$(225);
490      IF (48=INKEY(10)) THEN PROCfire(X)
500    UNTIL LEN(word$)=0
510    IF flag=TRUE THEN PROCship
520 NEXT K
530 END
540
550 DEF PROCfire(X)
560    FOR I=Y-2 TO 1 STEP -1
570      PRINT TAB(X,I)CHR$(226);
580      PRINT TAB(X,I+1) " ";
590    NEXT I
600    PRINT TAB(X,I+1) " ";
610    temp=ASC(LEFT$(word$,1)):word$=MID$(word$,2)
620    IF temp=91+X THEN PROChit(2) ELSE PROCmiss
630 ENDPROC
640
650 DEF PROChit(s)
660    score%=score%+s
670    VDU 19,0,9,0,0,0
680    SOUND 1,-15,53,30
690    z=INKEY(150)
700    VDU 19,0,4,0,0,0
710    PRINT TAB(24,30)score%
720 ENDPROC
730
740 DEF PROCmiss
750    SOUND 0,-15,44,10
760    flag=FALSE
770 ENDPROC
780
```

```
790 DEF PROCship
800    Z=0
810    REPEAT
820      Z=Z+1
830      PRINT TAB(Z,2) CHR$(224);
840      PRINT TAB(Z-1,2) " ";
850    UNTIL Z=39 OR 48=INKEY(10)
860    IF Z=39 ENDPROC
870    FOR I=Y-2 TO 2 STEP -1
880      PRINT TAB(X,I) CHR$(226);
890      PRINT TAB(X,I+1) " ";
900    NEXT I
910    PRINT TAB(X,I+1) " ";
920    IF X=Z THEN PROChit(10) ELSE REPEAT Z=Z+1:
       PRINT TAB(Z,2) CHR$(224);TAB(Z-1,2) " ";:
       q=INKEY(10):UNTIL Z=40
930    PRINT TAB(Z,2) " ";
940 ENDPROC
950
960 DATA man,car,police,computer,bus,cat
```

abcdefghijklmnopqrstuvwxyz

SCORE-

P100   Counting

This is a program which could have some use in the first
years of primary education. It displays a number of monsters
on the screen, and the user is required to count the
monsters and press the appropriate numeric key.

Only the numbers one through nine are used by the program,
the return key is not used.

The program can be used to keep five-year-olds quiet for a
little while.

COMMANDS

Key in program and type RUN.
Count the monsters and press the correct numeric key.

```
100 REM Program P100 - Counting
110 ENVELOPE 1,25,16,12,8,1,1,1,10,-100,0,-10,126,100
120 DIMX(10),Y(10)
130 count=RND(9)
140 MODE5
150 *FX9,10
160 *FX10,10
170 *FX 11,0
180 VDU 23,224,24,60,90,126,36,90,66,129
190 VDU 19,0,7;0;19,3,0;0;
200 COLOUR 1
210
220 X(1)=RND(19):Y(1)=RND(25)
230 FOR I=2 TO count
240    X(I)=RND(19):Y(I)=RND(25)
250    FOR J=1 TO I-1
260       IF X(I)=X(J) AND Y(I)=Y(J) THEN I=I-1
270    NEXT J
280 NEXT I
290
300 FOR I=1 TO count
310    PRINT TAB(X(I),Y(I)) CHR$(224)
320 NEXT I
330
```

```
340 REPEAT
350     flag=-1
360     PRINT TAB(0,28);
370     PRINT "How many monsters";
380     ans$=GET$
390     PRINT CHR$(11);SPC(26);CHR$(11);
400     ans=VAL(ans$)
410     IF ans=count THEN PROCcorrect
                     ELSE SOUND 0,-15,4,20:flag=0
420 UNTIL flag=-1
430
440 RUN
450 DEF PROCcorrect
460 VDU 19,0,13;0;
470 SOUND 1,1,53,50
480 X=INKEY(450)
490 VDU 19,0,7;0;
500 ENDPROC
```

How many monsters

BONUS PROGRAM

P101 School Report   MODEL B ONLY

This program prepares a school report on the printer for a student. The program could be developed to store data on tape and handle more than one student.

COMMANDS

Key in program.
Ensure printer is set up correctly then type RUN.
Enter details as requested.

```
100 REM Program P101 - School Report
110 MODE 7
120 PRINT "Please ensure that printer is ready "
130 PRINT "and that appropriate *FX commands have"
140 PRINT "been executed."
150 INPUT ''"Name of school "school$
160 school$=STRING$((60-LEN(school$)) DIV 2," ")+school$
170 INPUT '"Name of student "name$
180 VDU2:VDU1,13,1,10:VDU1,13,1,10:VDU1,13,1,10:VDU3
190 PROCsendline(school$)
200 VDU2:VDU1,13,1,10:VDU1,13,1,10:VDU1,13,1,10:VDU3
210 INPUT "Session "session$
220 PROCsendline("     School Report - "+session$)
230 PROCsendline("       Name:-    "+name$)
240 VDU1,13,1,10:VDU1,13,1,10:VDU1,13,1,10
250 PROCsendline
       ("    Subject   !Attend!Grade!Position!      Comment")
260 PROCsendline(STRING$(14," ")+
       "! P  A !     !in class!")
270 PROCsendline(STRING$(14,"_")+
       "!_____!_____!_____!"+STRING$(22,"_"))
280 REPEAT
290   INPUT "Subject (999 to end) "subject$
300   INPUT "Possible attendance "poss$
310   INPUT "Actual attendance "actual$
320   INPUT "Grade "grade$
330   INPUT "Position in class "position$
340   INPUT "Teacher's comment "comment$
350   IF subject$<>"999" THEN PROCprint
360 UNTIL subject$="999"
370 VDU2:VDU1,13,1,10:VDU1,13,1,10:VDU1,13,1,10:VDU3
380 PROCsendline("Overall Assessment")
390 PROCsendline(STRING$(18,"_"))
400 CLS
```

```
410 INPUT "Overall Assessment "line$
420 REPEAT
430    a$=LEFT$(line$,40)
440    line$=MID$(line$,41)
450    PROCsendline(a$)
460 UNTIL LEN(line$)=0
470 VDU2:VDU1,13,1,10:VDU1,13,1,10:VDU1,13,1,10:VDU3
480 PROCsendline("Signature of parent or guardian")
490 PROCsendline(STRING$(60,"_"))
500 END
510 DEF PROCprint
520    IF LEN(subject$)>14 THEN subject$=LEFT$(subject$,14)
530    subject$=subject$+STRING$(14-LEN(subject$)," ")
540    IF LEN(poss$)>3 THEN poss$=LEFT$(poss$,3)
550    poss$=poss$+STRING$(3-LEN(poss$)," ")
560    IF LEN(actual$)>3 THEN actual$=LEFT$(actual$,3)
570    actual$=actual$+STRING$(3-LEN(actual$)," ")
580    IF LEN(grade$)>5 THEN grade$=LEFT$(grade$,5)
590    grade$=grade$+STRING$(5-LEN(grade$)," ")
600    IF LEN(position$)>8 THEN position$=LEFT$(position$,8)
610    position$=position$+STRING$(8-LEN(position$)," ")
620    IF LEN(comment$)>20 THEN comment$=LEFT$(comment$,20)
630    line$=subject$+"!"+poss$+actual$+"!"+
                    grade$+"!"+position$+"!"+comment$
640    PROCsendline(line$)
650 ENDPROC
660 DEF PROCsendline(l$)
670    VDU2
680    FOR I=1 TO LEN(l$)
690       VDU 1,ASC(MID$(l$,I,1))
700    NEXT I
710    VDU 1,13
720    VDU1,10
730    VDU3
740 ENDPROC
```

Grangehill Comprehensive

School Report - 1983/84
Name:-   John Gordon

Subject	Attend P	A	Grade	Position in class	Comment
French	60	45	c	16	Inattentive
German	60	55	b	7	Good worker
Maths	60	55	f	23	Poor

Overall Assessment
_____

Could be better

Signature of parent or guardian
_____